Afrika Korps

Major K. J. Macksey, M.C.

BB

Editor-in-Chief: Barrie Pitt
Art Director: Peter Dunbar

Military Consultant: Sir Basil Liddell Hart
Picture Editor: Robert Hunt
Design Assistants: Gibson/Marsh
Christopher Lawton
David Eldred
Cover: Denis Piper
Research Assistant: Yvonne Marsh
Cartographers: Gatrell Ltd
Special Drawings: John Batchelor

Ballantine Books Inc.
101 Fifth Avenue, New York, NY 10003

'Company of soldiers

Introduction by Captain Sir Basil Liddell Hart

Rommel's name has become more famous than almost any of the chief actors in the Second World War, and through his fame the German Afrika Korps that he commanded in the North African campaigns has become as widely celebrated. The two are indelibly engraved in the pages of history. But less is known to the public about that body of troops than about Rommel himself, so it is valuable in every sense that the gap should now be filled by a book devoted primarily to the Afrika Korps, and providing a vivid account of its astonishing career in the desert – between its arrival at Tripoli in February 1941 and its ultimate liquidation in Tunisia two and a quarter years later, in May 1943.

When the first elements of the Afrika Korps reached Africa, in mid-February 1941, what was left of Marshal Graziani's large Italian army in Cyrenaica had just been cut off and captured at Beda Fomm the week before by the British mechanised force under General O'Connor. Such Italian forces as remained, in Tripolitania, were so shaken by the disastrous news as to be in no state to defend Italy's surviving foothold there. The first German transport ship arrived in Tripoli harbour on February 14, two days after Rommel himself had flown there. But it carried only two advanced units. Rommel hurried them up to the front – which at the moment was held by only a regiment of Italians – so as to create as much activity as possible to conceal his weakness and deter the British from following up their success by clearing the Italians out of Africa. It was not until almost mid-March that the Panzer regiment of his leading division disembarked at Tripoli, and even by the end of March the whole of that division –

the 5th Light, later rechristened the 21st Panzer – had not arrived. The second of his two divisions, the 15th Panzer, was not due until May.

Nevertheless he launched a probing counter-offensive at the end of March with his one (still incomplete) division of the Afrika Korps – sensing that the British, after their prolonged offensive drive through Cyrenaica, were exhausted and in process of reorganisation. Applying his tonic effect to his Italian allies he got them to support his advance with parts of three fresh divisions they had sent to Africa. The trial thrust proved even more successful than he had hoped, and he speedily exploited it, with such disrupting effect that within a fortnight he had swept the British out of all their recent gains in Cyrenaica, except the port of Tobruk, where he had surrounded most of what remained of their forces. Although his efforts to capture Tobruk failed, the balance of the war in Africa had been drastically changed.

In May and again in June the British launched renewed offensives with such fresh forces as had been sent to North Africa, but each time Rommel and the Afrika Korps succeeded in repelling them while still maintaining the investment of Tobruk. In November, after Auchinleck had replaced Wavell as Commander-in-Chief in the Middle East, the British launched a much larger offensive that Winston Churchill hoped would destroy the Afrika Korps and clear both the Germans and the Italians out of Africa. The British forces, now entitled the Eighth Army, outnumbered the Germans and Italians together by more than 9 to 4 in tanks, and the Germans – who were 'the backbone of the enemy's army', as Auchinleck emphasised – by more than 4 to 1. (Actually, the British total of gun-armed tanks was 756, with more than a third more in reserve, whereas the German total of gun-armed tanks was 174, and the Italians 146 – of an obsolescent type.) Yet in this 'Operation Crusader', it was only by the sheer attrition of superior numbers, after a prolonged touch-and-go struggle, that Rommel and his forces were driven to withdraw from Cyrenaica to the border of Tripolitania – from which they had advanced in the spring.

A month later, after the belated arrival of a fresh convoy that brought its depleted tank strength up from 50 to 100 tanks, the Afrika ·Korps hit back, shattered a newly arrived British armoured division, and regained the Gazala Line in eastern Cyrenaica by the beginning of February. Then in May Rommel forestalled a fresh British offensive by his own stroke at the Gazala Line. This time he had 280 German gun-armed tanks, with 230 obsolescent Italian, against nearly 1,000 British. Moreover the British now had 167 American Grant tanks with a heavier punch than any except 19 of his own. Yet after a fortnight's battling, the superior skill of the Afrika Korps was so marked that the balance had changed hands. Tobruk had been taken by storm, and the remains of the Eighth Army were driven back in helter-skelter retreat to the Alaméin Line, its last shelter before the Nile Delta. Only there were Rommel and his very tired men at last brought to a halt.

Throughout this dramatic year and a quarter, the Afrika Korps comprised only its original two small divisions (of 2 tank and 3 infantry battalions apiece), plus an improvised light division that Rommel had formed out of a few odd infantry and artillery units. Only after he was stopped at Alamein did Hitler fly in another German infantry division to help him. He had also had six weak Italian divisions, but of these only one was mechanised and one motorised (although two more arrived as reinforcements at Alamein they were ill-equipped).

It was only when Montgomery took over command of the Eighth Army in August, and when its superiority of strength over the Germans was increased to the vast odds of over 6 to 1 in tanks – and in aircraft – that the scales finally turned against Rommel, and the Afrika Korps was finally worn down. Even then the remnant of it carried out a 2,000-mile retreat to Tunis, in six months, without ever being cut off by its greatly superior pursuers, and was only trapped at last when the Allied-dominated sea lay at its back.

Rommel's small force, basically composed of the Afrika Korps, had drawn into the North African theatre the equivalent of more than 20 divisions from Britain's strength – nearly half her operational strength. In essence, that was the supreme testimony to its effect as a strategic distraction – the core of the story that Kenneth Macksey tells so well.

Early in 1942 Winston Churchill in the House of Commons did honour to Rommel in a tribute such as has rarely been paid to an enemy in time of war: 'We have a very daring and skilful opponent against us, and, may I say across the havoc of war, a great general'. That tribute might as justly be paid to the Afrika Korps itself, using the term 'great soldiers', and be all the more unhesitatingly set on record in the light of history.

African sideshow

Italian colonists of Tripolitania lived their daily lives in something like panic in early February 1941, and the reason was plain to see – the Italian Army, or what remained of it, trembled on the wings of a crushing defeat, and those who survived no longer had heart for the fight. And not just in Tripolitania did the Italians show signs of collapse: in East Africa their colonial army had been overwhelmed and was stumbling towards total dissolution, while in Albania a Mussolini inspired invasion which, in November, had started forth to conquer Greece, now clung to whatever strongholds it could against a Greek counter-offensive that threatened to repeat what the British had done in Africa.

Moreover, between the homeland and Tripolitania, the aggressive British-held island of Malta interposed air and sea strikes against the convoys that endeavoured to rebuild Axis strength in Tripolitania, and although under constant attack from the Luftwaffe and Regia Aeronautica, it persistently kept the armies in North Africa in short supply. So when the Italian citizens heard their soldiers talk openly of packing their bags and returning helter-skelter to Europe, leaving them at the mercy of the indigenous Arabs, their fears multiplied, for little sympathy could be expected from that direction.

But, on this occasion, neither for love of conquest nor for altruistic reasons – the German Reich Chancellor, Adolf Hitler, decided to assist his Axis partner, the strutting Benito Mussolini. Outright victory in Europe, undisguised disdain for the poor showing of his ally, and an acute appraisal that rising German power was not inexhaustible (particularly in view of his recent decision to invade the Balkans and Russia that year) were all factors affecting the situation, but Hitler also knew that he could not permit a total Italian collapse anywhere, since to do so would expose the whole Axis southern flank to British seaborne attack, and might eventually undermine the structure of his own newly won Empire. Italy, needing assistance, would receive help, but only in sufficient strength to stabilise her existing frontiers. Henceforward Germany had increasingly to aid her weaker partner, wondering, at times, if it might not have been better for Italy to have remained neutral from the outset.

To the anxious Italian colonists the landing of a Heinkel 111 bomber at Castel Benito on February 12 merely represented another of the fleet of German aircraft which, for several days, had been flying back and forth from Sicily in the process of establishing a Luftwaffe base close to Tripoli. The presence of German service units had a reassuring effect – rather more than the unhappy, freshly shipped, elements of Xth Italian Corps, with the undergunned tanks of its Ariete Armoured Division, that passed on their way to the crumbling front in the east. From that Heinkel, however, there stepped a German general, slight in stature, keen but open in countenance, quick and dynamic in speech and manner, who was soon to change the whole course of events in North Africa.

This was Erwin Rommel, the man who, as

a junior officer, had helped break the Italians at Caporetto in 1917, who had witnessed the German victory in Poland in 1939 as commander of Hitler's personal escort, and who, in France in 1940, had led 7th Panzer Division with outstanding dash and verve to play a leading part in the destruction of the Anglo-French Armies. And now he stood, virtually on the edge of the desert, his mind balancing a natural inclination to attack at the first possible opportunity, against a directive from Hitler and Field-Marshal von Brauchitsch, forbidding him to take offensive action until a complete German armoured corps had been shipped in. In the reckoning, too, weighed the fears of the Italian Commando Supremo in Rome that the British would sweep on to conquer the whole of Tripolitania, plus the orders forbidding the Luftwaffe to bomb Benghazi because of the danger to Italian civilian officials still living there.

Rommel believed that mechanised warfare demanded constant movement and that a defensive posture in no way forbade local offensive actions within the framework of the main defence. But much depended, of course, on what the British might do before he could begin to develop his strategy.

General Wavell's Desert Army had reached El Agheila after a demonstration of supreme desert mobility using light (and at times provocatively small) mechanised forces that had become, by intensive practice, a thoroughly acclimatised desert elite. For all that the Italians or Rommel could see, they might easily continue to come straight along the coast to Tripoli, because early in February no sizeable force could be placed in their way; and an Italian plan to defend the Buerat position halfway between Agheila and Tripoli, represented more a wish than a hope. Already long range British patrols were known to be probing deep into Tripolitania, the forerunners, perhaps, of another lunge forward by the main body.

Yet now, as he nearly always did, Rommel planned intuitively while in possession of only the sparsest information about the enemy. Only vaguely could he be aware that the *coup de grace* executed upon Graziani's Army by the British Lt-General O'Connor at Beda Fomm on February 7 had been at the hands of only 32 cruiser tanks and 3,000 men: he could only surmise that even this effort had totally exhausted the British who, in fact, were in the process of establishing a static defence in Cyrenaica (backed by woefully inadequate armoured forces), while shipping whatever could be spared to Greece to honour a political obligation given to a gallant but weakening ally.

At the back of Rommel's mind must have lain concern that German mobile forces,

Erwin Rommel

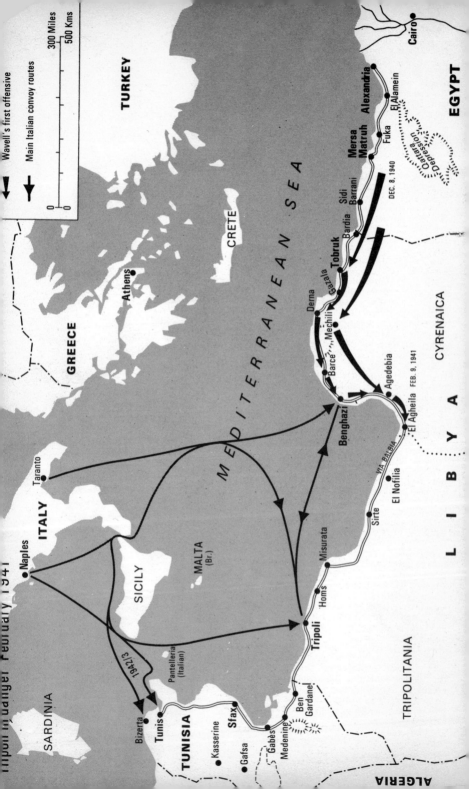

The debris of an Army. Italian equipment litters the battlefield after the British victory in late 1940

pitchforked from their European environment into an entirely new situation at the shortest possible notice, might fail for technical if not psychological reasons. The desert posed many imponderables for those unaccustomed to its habits: like a woman it could brood and be highly temperamental, was given to sudden storms and moments of tranquil beauty – and quite often it won a man's heart so that, as he strove to overcome its vicissitudes, a deep rooted affection or a baffled rage overcame him.

Mostly its surface was a waterless waste, hot by day and, in winter, bitterly cold. Natural vegetation grew profusely mostly only where the Italian colonists had irrigated and farmed with neat efficiency along the coastal strip in the neighbourhood of the principal towns, although in the hinterland, wells supported a few nomadic tribes and saved many a lost traveller from death by thirst. In this arid land man had to carry what he needed and nothing did he need more than water.

Nowhere could it be said that any particular topographical feature dominated. Various escarpments such as that by Halfaya on the Egyptian border, salt marshes such as those running south of the desert west of El Agheila and the Qattara Depression south of El Alamein, and great sand-seas of soft going, scattered about, canalised movement in a land that boasted only one main coastal road plus a multitude of uncertain inland tracks. To supply forces operating close to the coast presented infinitely fewer problems than just a few miles inland. Coastal movement drew from the road and the ports: inland movement depended upon accurate navigation by wheeled or tracked vehicles manned by men who, even when fully acclimatised to the desert, more often than not thoroughly disliked it. Hence sense of direction lost meaning, sandstorms could obliterate landmarks and the mirage made a mockery of judging distance.

Rommel had much to learn and little time in which to learn it: the same applied to his men. Indeed the very fact that the Italians possessed greater desert experience than the Germans, prompted General Gariboldi, Chief of Staff in Rome, to talk down to Rommel and, thereby, provoke the latter to even greater aggression. A suggestion by Gariboldi that Rommel could hardly be expected to have an idea of the

difficulties of the country, drew forth the retort 'It won't take me long to get to know . . . I'll have a look at it from the air this afternoon and report back to the High Command this evening.'

Yet Gariboldi judged well – if in safety. Desert conditions, the dust, the loneliness of the empty void, navigational problems and the mirage, were but a few of the phenomena which could impose unheard of destructive strains on men and machines. It was not as if Rommel's embryonic command – the Afrika Korps – had time to gather itself together. The advance guard, 5th Light Division, was newly formed – a grafting from 3rd Panzer Division – and operating on a reduced establishment to the conventional panzer division. It possessed only one armoured brigade, the 5th, of two tank battalions adding up to 150 tanks, supported by three infantry battalions, artillery and the 3rd Reconnaissance Battalion. Rommel commented with pride on Italian enthusiasm at the sight of the excellent German equipment, but, in fact, only 80 of the tanks were the powerful Mark III and IV type (causing Rommel to feel the need to disguise some Volkswagens to look like tanks) and, although the versa-

tility of the German machinery brooked no dispute in Europe, there had been too little time to adapt it to desert conditions. The extremes of operating conditions were to impose breaking loads on the German armour and Rommel, an infantryman, had less sympathy with the mechanics than might a tank general. For that reason he often demanded more than was feasible – and sometimes got it!

Let there be no doubt that the Afrika Korps, although much smaller in numbers than the Italian Army in Tripolitania, carried the full weight of the Axis burden from the moment it landed in Africa. Later it was to increase to two Panzer Divisions, when 15th Panzer Division arrived and 5th Light was to be given full status and rechristened 21st Panzer. Later still other German formations, notably 90th Light Division, were to come under command.

Afrika Korps represented, from the start, the hub and driving force behind every Axis move in the desert. Wherever it went the battle flared fiercest: when it hid from view the British paused in doubt, but once in view it had to be reckoned with as the epicentre of eruption.

13

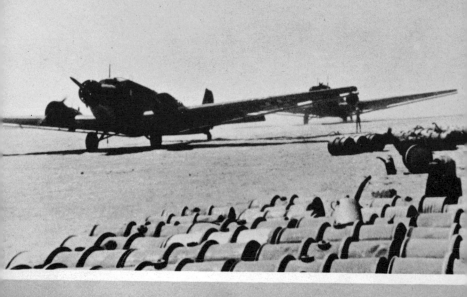

JU 52's unloading at Castel Benito

Pz Kw II tanks on their way to the front

First offensive: the run of luck

The leading elements of Afrika Korps landed at Tripoli on February 14. By then Rommel had flown his reconnaissance and, with Mussolini's approval, taken command of all troops at the front. That same day the first Italian units were ordered off to the front at Sirte, to be followed within 24 hours by the German 3rd Reconnaissance Battalion and an anti-tank battalion, reaching Sirte on the 16th. Already Rommel had decided 'to depart from my instructions to confine myself to reconnaissance', so it is not surprising to learn that the first brush with a British patrol took place at Nofilia on the 28th – 75 miles beyond Sirte.

From that moment Rommel expanded his intuitive evaluation of British intentions, their repeatedly negative response to his provocations convincing him that no further advance to the west need be expected. Armed with this opinion he flew to Berlin on March 19 (just after the whole of 5th Panzer Regiment had landed and started for the front) to seek Hitler's permission to undertake the recapture of all Cyrenaica – having already given orders for preliminary moves against El Agheila before his departure. He met however, with a cool reception. Brauchitsch announced that there was no intention of striking a decisive blow in Africa in the near future, that no additional resources to those already earmarked were to be sent, but that, at the end of May, an attack might be made against El Agheila – after 15th Panzer Division had arrived. Nobody told Rommel of the plans to invade the Balkans

or Russia (it is likely that he would have been deeply depressed had he known), but from the start the treatment by Berlin of this 'Desert side-show' left no doubt that Afrika Korps would forever be starved of aid and never integrated into the major Axis strategy. Nevertheless, Rommel returned to Africa with his mind fixed on the illicit attack against El Agheila and on March 24 was able to report that, not only had it fallen, but that the British had withdrawn to the next defile, at Mersa Brega. His optimisim fermented – if only because he had done what Berlin had forbidden for another two months.

Rommel and his Afrika Korps, learning their trade apace in long desert marches and short, carefully limited actions, might have felt still greater elation had they been aware of the true state of affairs in the British camp. Whatever British resources could be withdrawn from the desert had returned to the Nile Delta, the victorious leaders and some of the men to have a rest, others for despatch to new fronts. In their place stood untried troops under inexperienced commanders whose plans neither fitted the ground they hoped to defend nor the character of the enemy they were destined to meet. General Wavell, his attention distracted by a multitude of crises accruing from a host of battlefronts throughout the length and breadth of his command, could not give to any the attention that they deserved.

Of course Wavell had to show confidence in his subordinate commanders, but Lieutenant-General Wilson, before his

5th Panzer Regiment on the desert road

Rommel's aerial command post – the Storch

departure for Greece, imparted a totally false impression of the defensible strength of the escarpment south of Benghazi. Lieutenant-General Neame, who took over from Wilson, seemed to lack confidence and proposed tactical plans that were impracticable: and Wavell's intelligence staff produced only fragmentary information about the German build-up. In fact, the British Director of Intelligence suggested that a sudden foray by Afrika Korps into Cyrenaica might happen, but Wavell, as sound, practical and orthodox a commander as Brauchitsch, rejected that possibility until May. Normal military commonsense, he thought, precluded so hazardous an undertaking.

In manpower and material the British position looked hardly more promising. The only elements capable of survival in a mobile desert battle are acclimatised, mechanised and, preferably, armoured, formations. The British 2nd Armoured Division, however, took its title more in name than actuality for its units (with one exception) were new to the desert, its cruiser and light tanks worn out – and the one experienced regiment that had just been rushed up from the Delta was only given a number of sub-standard Italian M13 tanks that had been captured at Beda Fomm. The best infantry formation was the Australian 9th Division, but it had yet to prove itself and, in any case, had to detach one of its three brigades in Tobruk to put the old Italian defences in order, partly because the scale of administrative support could not be stretched to supply more than 2nd Armoured Division and two infantry brigades in advance of Benghazi.

To a certain extent the weakness of the British dispositions was divined by Rommel, as a result of intercepts of radio traffic,

the lack of positive reaction to his probes, the paucity of air activity (the Royal Air Force only mustered two fighter, one bomber and an Army Co-operation Squadron in the desert at that time) and the information garnered by his own small, but efficient air component. Encouraged at every turn, 5th Light Division assaulted Mersa Brega on March 31 and, for the first time, came up against a tough core of resistance supplied by a British infantry battalion, a regiment of 25-pounder field artillery and a regiment of anti-tank guns.

Rommel had fought the British in France the previous May and learnt to respect their tenacity: 3rd Panzer Division, the parent of 5th Light, had met only the French in that campaign and found them much easier meat. By late afternoon the crisis arrived, with 5th Light held up in the 8 mile gap between the marsh and the sea, and the British commander, aware that his men fought at their last gasp, calling for a counter-attack by the tanks of 3rd Armoured Brigade. 5th Light were busy organising a fresh effort, their tanks groping about in the thick dust flung up by tracks and gunfire: for a moment they were off balance. But Major-General Gambier-Parry, commanding 2nd Armoured Division, declined to release his armoured brigade because he considered time too short before nightfall: instead he had to conform to Afrika Korps' next attack and withdraw from the defensive neck.

Three vital psychological milestones had been passed in just a few hours. The British had been driven out of one of the few really narrow defensive positions close to the coast and must now, with weak mobile forces, fight a vastly stronger enemy in the open desert. Secondly, the Afrika Korps had won its first battle against a sturdy foe

Afrika Korps enters Benghazi

and thereby found its feet, established self-confidence and braced itself for anything that might come. Above all, Rommel had proved, what earlier he had only surmised, that his enemy stood ripe for jostling: not only need he not wait for the end of May to attack El Agheila - perhaps the whole of Cyrenaica lay at his feet. The British were bent on withdrawal - he would follow.

On April 2 he reached Agedabia, meditating which of three alternative routes he might next take. One ran due north to Benghazi, a supply and distribution centre protected by the escarpment; a second east and then north east towards Mechili via Tengeder far in the enemy rear; and a third, bisecting the other two, to Msus and thence also to Mechili. The rules of war - such as they can be in relation to an art - prescribe that a commander should not split his force in the face of an undefeated enemy. Rommel threw the book to the winds and divided 5th Light Division all three ways, at the same time calling forward the Italian infantry divisions to take over the regained territory while mixing the Italian mobile units with the German hard core. Thus he established a moving base to follow the racing, mobile striking force - Afrika Korps.

Ahead, the British Generals eased his passage when Wavell introduced split responsibility in the chain of command. Arriving at Neame's headquarters at Barce and drawing the conclusion that Neame had lost control of the battle, Wavell ordered O'Connor - the victor of Beda Fomm - out of convalescence back to the desert to take over: simultaneously he cancelled his original instruction to give up Benghazi if necessary. This divided 2nd Armoured Division against Gambier-Parry's desire to stay concentrated, for on April 2 his Support Group had to be detached, at Wavell's behest, to cover Benghazi. In any case 3rd Armoured Brigade had only 22 cruisers and 25 light tanks left and, on Gambier-Parry's estimate, would lose one by breakdown for every 10 miles run. Furthermore O'Connor, loath to take over in the midst of a battle, agreed only to act as Neame's adviser.

On the few occasions tank met tank, honours ended fairly even - the use of Bedouin tents to conceal British cruiser tanks teaching the Afrika Korps that subterfuge has as much a place in the desert as elsewhere, but Rommel pressing forward with irresistible ardour, overbore every vestige of opposition - even amongst his Allies. To Gariboldi, anxious to curb a headlong rush, Rommel plainly stated that he had 'no intention of allowing good opportunities to slip by unused', and rejected the Italian's proposal to refer the matter to Rome. Fortunately the disagreement melted almost at once upon receipt of a signal from the malleably opportunist, if not overwhelmingly foresighted, German High Command giving Rommel a free hand.

British opposition declined. Concurrently the cloying, inherent initial weaknesses of the Afrika Korps appeared. Tanks running in totally foreign conditions needed an overhaul every 1,500 miles in-

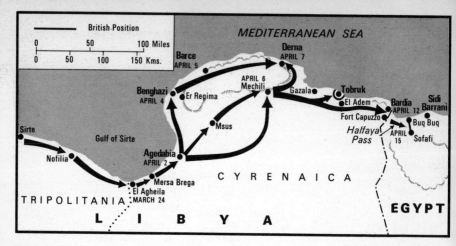

stead of at twice that distance; dragging petrol to the leading troops imposed a fearful strain, but when General Streich, the commander of 5th Light Division, reported on April 3 that he needed four days to bring up enough petrol to continue the advance, he was sharply told to unload all his vehicles, top them up with more fuel and to move on in 24 hours. In the midst of battle Rommel trained his Korps to the standard of performance that had become 'normal' in his old 7th Panzer Division the year before. The men, grumbling but proud in victory, laboured with redoubled energy to satisfy the demands of a man who commanded from the air, or in a light vehicle bounding ahead at the apex of the leading troops. Many who became lost, or who crawled instead of raced, found themselves at the receiving end of a tirade when a fuming Rommel landed alongside in his light aircraft.

On April 4 the triple-pronged offensive slid forward practically unchecked, two of its spikes forking either side of the disintegrating 2nd Armoured Division, isolating it from east and west. 3rd Reconnaissance Battalion entered Benghazi unopposed, confronted by blazing British stores; but on turning east ran full tilt into an Australian battalion, supported by 25-pounders at Er Regima, and suffered a brusque repulse. Fanning out from Agedabia the other two Axis columns made their separate ways towards Mechili, each a self-sufficient battlegroup of tanks, guns and infantry capable of undertaking almost any combat task short of a prolonged assault against a well prepared position. Along the furthest inland route went the 'Ariete' Armoured Division, following a track described by an Italian General as 'a death trap', but which Rommel took himself because he, 'placed more faith in my own observation'. He judged well and this group, commanded by Lieutenant-Colonel

Schwerin, soon developed into the greatest threat of all to the British – far more than Colonel Olbrich's column on the track to Msus where bad going and the associated high expenditure of petrol exacted its penalty. On April 6 Schwerin arrived at Mechili, far in the British rear, lonely, but not in danger.

The 2nd British Armoured Division had practically ceased to exist, so only 9th Australian Division lay west of Mechili and could do but one thing – retreat as fast as possible within the perimeter of Tobruk. Mechili, Rommel discovered, was held by the 3rd Indian Motorised Brigade (an infantry group almost devoid of anti-tank weapons) supplemented by stragglers. Indeed all over the desert men and vehicles lay dotted about and mixed up, friend amongst foe. Once Rommel himself nearly landed his Storch alongside a British column mistaking it for one of his own: but at Mechili, and along the road to Derna, the German bag filled with captive British generals – all except Morshead of 9th Australian Division. Even O'Connor was amongst them and Gambier-Parry joined the party when a sortie from Mechili failed, leaving the Indians no alternative except surrender.

By April 7, British control of the Middle East was in jeopardy. Their desert defensive flank had crumbled in ruins, only 9th Australian Division and some scratched together armour and artillery held the port of Tobruk while, eastward, the road to the main base in Egypt yawned wide open and undefended. Of course, Afrika Korps – or rather, 5th Light Division – was almost exhausted too, with much of its complement strung out bogged—broken-down or out of petrol on the tracks leading back to Agedabia. By all the rules both sides needed a halt, but the strategic situation allowed it to neither. British reinforcement priority had to shift at once from Greece to

Captured British generals – O'Connor centre, Gambier-Parry right.
The rank and file – British and Indian prisoners sharing rations

Cyrenaica; and Rommel could not afford to stand still and lose momentum or initiative.

Halting or resting thus became a luxury that Afrika Korps got used to being denied – like the ballerina wearing magic shoes who could not stop dancing once the music began. Sweating and straining, Afrika Korps' scattered remnants closed up to Mechili, followed by the Italians and joined on April 10 by the advanced guard of 15th Panzer Division – its commander Major-General von Prittwitz. Not for him a leisurely acclimatisation either, for Rommel was certain by April 10 that the British were in collapse and that, once Tobruk fell into his hands and provided a secure entrance for his supplies, no obstacle would bar a direct advance to the Suez Canal. The precipitate haste with which he picked up his still breathless divisions seemed entirely justified by an instinctive belief that only by constant relentless pressure could the perilously unbalanced British be kept on the run. Moreover, the Luftwaffe had detected the signs of regeneration in the Tobruk defensive perimeter – so, full throttle, Rommel aimed for Tobruk, placing von Prittwitz in charge of the operation. But tired, disorganised men are most prone to unnecessary errors and now the exertions of the past week wore away the previous sharp edge of Afrika Korps.

Third Reconnaissance Battalion, followed by the rest of 5th Light, Italian 'Brescia' and then 'Ariete' Divisions, arrived piecemeal outside Tobruk, on April 10-11, feeling their way clumsily and tentatively round the perimeter, bumping into roving bands of Australian defenders here and there, and losing von Prittwitz who was killed in an early skirmish. Even Rommel had to admit that the situation had become rather confused, and spent the rest of the 11th at the front organising the next attack himself. Time and events, however, were leaving him behind.

The Australians had taken over a stronger proposition than might have been expected. Stocks of water, ammunition and food within the garrison ran high, and the work carried out by the reserve Australian Brigade made good sense. Now they waited, four brigades of them, the remnants of 3rd Armoured Brigade with 23 cruisers and some light tanks, four regiments of 25-pounder guns, enough anti-aircraft artillery to make the harbour area unpleasant for dive-bombers and even a squadron of Hurricane fighters, for a while, to give the defenders yet more opportunity to ship in supplies partly unmolested.

On the frontier, too, a new mobile force gathered under Brigadier Gott, based on Halfaya Pass and charged with the job of raiding towards Tobruk in the hope that this might distract Rommel from his main objective. For the moment Rommel could only suffer these pin-pricks in anger, and

take note that Halfaya Pass must be his at the earliest opportunity. First of all, Tobruk must be taken – but the first headlong rush on the 11th got nowhere – and for good reason.

The British defensive system, all 30 miles of it, could never be held in a linear fashion by so small a force as that within. A resilient, mobile defence, based on strong points, set amongst minefields, alone offered success. To defeat a system such as that demands the careful selection of the place of entry, followed by concentration of all resources upon that point while diversionary activities distract the enemy's attention and delude him as to the real place and time of impact. Rommel admitted that he had no idea of the extent of the defences of the British positions and that his every act became an improvisation.

Finding part of 5th Light to the south of Tobruk, he whipped it round to the east to close the ring completely. Next he gathered 5th Panzer Regiment and flung it pell-mell straight up the road towards El Adem, under a volley of protests from its commander Colonel Olbrich. But Rommel brushed such doubts aside and travelled with the tanks himself until they ran into a storm of fire covering the approaches to an anti-tank ditch. That stopped that rush: meanwhile on the western perimeter face a half-hearted push by 'Brescia' barely got beyond its start line. Nevertheless, the siege lines now ran fully round the landward approaches to Tobruk, with the Luftwaffe beginning to tighten its attacks on shipping entering and leaving the harbour.

Waiting three days to re-gather and prepare his men, Rommel next launched 5th Light and 'Ariete' into the sort of assault which, in France, had never failed – a solid phalanx of armour and infantry, supported by artillery fire, advancing on a narrow front with all guns blazing. The French had wilted before this treatment, but the Australians stood firm. Moreover, the all-too obvious (because it was hasty) reconnaissance leading up to the attack, left the defenders in no doubt where the main effort would come.

From the start everything went wrong for 5th Light: Ariete did not arrive in time to widen the base of the assault and then the primary, deep penetration achieved by the armour ran straight into a cauldron of shell-fire, supporting skilful flank attacks by British tanks and anti-tank guns. To Olbrich the shock and the rapid loss of 17 tanks came too hard. He withdrew, leaving the infantry to their fate, convincing even Rommel that, for the moment, nothing more could be done – a lesson rubbed home later that day when the laggard 'Ariete' bolted in confusion the moment they arrived at the front.

For the first time, Afrika Korps was seized by doubts. They lay at the end of extended lines of communication, bereft of

Italy's obsolescent M.13 tanks

23

adequate reinforcements, side-by-side with an ally of the most doubtful quality: one weakened division against a resurgent opponent. On April 11, 3rd Reconnaissance Battalion, under Colonel von Herff, had reached Bardia, but suffered from then on from the waspish attentions of Brigadier Gott. 'Ariete', trying to redeem its reputation by a solo assault at Tobruk on April 16, stopped at the first sign of an Australian counter-attack and ran, to Rommel's disgust, 'towards the British lines'. Every night, aggressive patrols crept out from the garrison to disturb the composure of the Germans and Italians of the besieging force, and in a day or two these led to sizeable raids inflicting serious losses on the latter. The initiative had passed to the British; only by restoring Afrika Korps as an independent mobile reserve could equilibrium be assured.

As quickly as possible, Italian divisions were fed into the line at Tobruk and 5th Light withdrawn for rest and refitting close by to await the arrival of the first echelons of 15th Panzer Division. However, almost immediately, the situation near Halfaya Pass became too hot for von Herff, who panicked and persuaded Rommel that his troops at Bardia and Capuzzo were in danger of being cut off. Consequently the newly arrived and barely acclimatised 15th Motorised Light Infantry Battalion found itself in action for the first time alongside 3rd Reconnaissance Battalion in a sharp little fight that drove Gott, helter-skelter, out of Halfaya Pass.

The front simmered, Rommel fumed at the Italians and the Italians responded by convincing Hitler (and Rommel) that no advance into Egypt stood the remotest chance of success until Tobruk had been taken. The German General Staff in Berlin, a fortnight ago happy to give Rommel a free hand, now had a feeling things were in a mess, General Halder noting, 'His motor vehicles are in poor condition and many of the tank engines need replacing . . . Air transport cannot meet his senseless demands, primarily because of lack of fuel . .' and sent General Paulus, the Deputy Chief of the General Staff, to examine and report. Everybody vented their wrath on the Italians, not only because of their poor performance in the desert, but also because the movement of troops and supplies in Italian ships across the Mediterranean had grown so slow and hazardous. Vehicles and stores choked Naples, waiting for transport: but the British Royal Navy lay omnipotently across the sea lanes and on April 12, amongst other successes, sank the entire Signal Reserve Battalion of 15th Panzer Division.

Into the midst of the torrid heat now stepped the cold presence of General Paulus, bent on putting the headstrong amateur right and, above all, ensuring that never again would Rommel stampede his superiors into a wasteful side-show.

Pz Kw IV with L/24 75mm gun
The main battle tank of the Wehrmacht for the first part of the Second World War and of Afrika Korps for almost its entire career. The earlier versions, shown here, had a low velocity gun as their main armament, with a muzzle velocity of only 1263 feet per second, and armour that could easily be pierced by British guns. Its ability to fire at greater ranges than the 2-pounder armed British tanks, nevertheless, conferred a transitory tactical advantage that was of lesser importance than the fundamental soundness of design that permitted significant increases in protection and striking power to be made at later dates.
Weight: 20 tons. Speed: 25 MPH.
Armour (max): 30 mm Crew: 5.
Armament: 1 x 75 mm gun, 2 x 7·9 mm mg

Summer 1941: the point of balance

Success has a nasty habit of recoiling against its creators, for once it becomes public property, the public expect encores. Even amidst the clamour of sweeping victories in the Balkans, the name of Rommel and his Afrika Korps reverberated in Germany as the Propaganda Machine took hold – leading to a protest by Rommel at the ravings of one hack writer whose imagination ran wilder than the rest. But Paulus took a cool look, and on April 27 vetoed a proposal to attack Tobruk again on the 30th – reversing the ban only 24 hours before H Hour. In the meantime, 15th Panzer Division began to arrive in greater strength while the Afrika Korps as a whole underwent intensive training in the sort of positional warfare at which the British had proved so superior, but in which the Germans failed for lack of foresight. Yet the sacking of Streich, the commander of 5th Light, and his replacement by General Kirchheim ushered in no profound change in the method of command, for it was Rommel who dominated – he who inspired all levels.

On April 29 a concentrated aerial and artillery bombardment fell on the sector chosen for assault, alerting the Australians who, in any case, could watch Afrika Korps and 'Ariete' forming up in their assembly area. Thus when the attack went in on the 30th, the reception was hotter than ever, both sides becoming mixed up in a turmoil of dust, with neither fully aware of what was taking place at the point of impact. Again, however, the limitations of the Afrika Korps were laid bare, for the attention to

training in positional warfare now led them into costly attacks on each and any Australian post, of several that held out. So, instead of exploiting an early penetration in depth, the assault stuck in the crust of the perimeter mine-field and became swallowed up by the voracious appetite of numerous individual combats; and when at last the armour attempted to break through near Ras el Medauar, it came into contact with British tanks, swapped casualties and halted. On May 1 the attack was renewed but with little progress against a dogged defence and in the face of fierce artillery bombardments. Moreover, the Australians, on launching strong counter-attacks, finally convinced Rommel – and above all Paulus – that the Axis lacked the strength to overcome Tobruk at that time.

An ominous indication of defeat emerges in Rommel's letter to his wife on May 6, where it talks of shortage of water at Tobruk, and complains of the effects of the heat, the desert wind and his own unquenchable thirst – something that betokens the misery of many of his men. Paulus recommended to Halder, with the concurrence of Rommel and the Italian Command, that a halt must be called, Halder complaining that, 'Rommel has brought about a situation for which our present supply capabilities are insufficient.' But respite was the one thing the British were not prepared to grant Afrika Korps.

The sequence of British success in the Mediterranean had ended with the Battle of Matapan on March 28. Evacuation from Greece had done little to strengthen Egypt

since what little material that had been saved went to Crete. However, a few tanks could be dredged out of workshops and depots and sent to the Cyrenaican frontier. Meanwhile, the British Prime Minister, Mr Churchill, had on his own responsibility despatched a convoy filled with aircraft and armoured vehicles to run the gauntlet through the Mediterranean, to infuse new strength into Wavell's depleted forces. But the 'Tiger' convoy, as it was known, would not arrive until May 12 (eight days before the German airborne attack on Crete took place) and its contents, at best, could not be ready for action until June 7 – and even by then it seemed unlikely that the tank crews would be properly trained to use new types of vehicles.

Wavell could not wait that long, He knew that a new Panzer Division – the 15th – would get to the desert before the contents of the Tiger Convoy. In any case, Wavell surmised that the Germans were weak at Halfaya and, knowing that their armour still lay close to Tobruk, calculated that Halfaya could be overrun and – a long shot – that Tobruk might be relieved. Operations such as these, carried out by only weak forces (and Brigadier Gott only had 29 old cruisers and 26 heavy Matilda tanks to support the equivalent of two infantry brigades) depend above all upon surprise. Unfortunately for him, Operation 'Brevity' – Wavell's spoiling attack – did not enjoy this vital advantage.

Long before the first shot of the attack was fired on May 15, Rommel had interpreted a Reuter Press Agency report that

all German troops had been driven out of Egypt, as a warning. At once he earmarked an extra panzer battalion to reinforce the frontier the moment the British attack appeared, although this did nothing to save the bulk of von Herff's group from extinction. For the Matilda tanks proving, as Rommel had seen in France, almost impervious to gunfire, ground through Halfaya on to Sollum and then to Fort Capuzzo, inexorably crushing a company of 15th Motorised Light Infantry battalion and the Italian infantry and artillery that ineffectually blocked the way. At Capuzzo a battalion of British infantry entered the fort only to receive a severe buffeting from a furious counter-attack by Herff's armour – a counter-attack that was then, itself, taken in rear by the Matildas. These armoured encounters introduced a new pattern, for, to their consternation, the German tank crews saw their shot fail to disable the Matildas, whereas the latter's 2-pounder guns quite often penetrated their tanks with ease. From this moment, therefore, Afrika Korps's tank crews acted with reticence and quite often the British crews found difficulty keeping their worn out machines running long enough to get within range of an enemy who frequently refused action.

Meanwhile the fresh panzer reinforcement from Tobruk approached the British cruisers which, swinging earlier round the desert flank, had already established themselves at Sidi Azeiz. To escape from between the British at Capuzzo and Sidi Azeiz, von Herff also moved to join the rein-

left: Defeat, a British Matilda tank driver surrenders at pistol point
Tension, Afrika Korps infantry take cover

left: Supply – motor tyres
Supply – water, essential for drinking, a luxury for washing

The spoils of victory – knocked out Matilda tanks

forcement – not knowing that the British commander, Gott, had told the cruisers at Sidi Azeiz to retreat during the night for fear of being swamped by the threat from Tobruk. Both parties passed undetected in opposite directions in the dark and next day, to their mutual surprise, found the battlefield empty. And at that moment, as the panzers from Tobruk reached Sidi Azeiz, they ran out of petrol – a revealing anti-climax.

To the British, the only territorial gain from Operation 'Brevity' was Halfaya Pass. The strength of enemy reaction had surprised them: they were not to know how shaken the Afrika Korps tank crews were or how heavy were the losses suffered by 15th Motorised Battalion. But, they might have guessed how vital Halfaya was to Rommel and could possibly have done much more to garrison the area and protect its flank. Indeed, Rommel considered that without possession of Halfaya, his tenure of positions outside Tobruk lived in pawn: the pass had to be retaken at once and then permanently held.

The exploitation of victory – a captured Crusader put to Afrika Korps's use

By now, in fact, Rommel's strength exceeded that of the British, whose new armour still lay stripped in Delta workshops or working-up in the hands of new crews. His quick, heavy attack launched from the head of Halfaya Pass and round its flank on May 27, pinned the British garrison down and gave the nine unhappy Matildas no chance to manoeuvre against such an overwhelming force. Pleased with possession of the Pass, the destruction of half the defenders and a pile of recaptured Italian equipment Rommel ordered its full scale fortification, impressing several Italian guns for the purpose, and went to see for himself that it was well done.

And at that moment he got a surprise message from General Gariboldi, informing him that only Italians could be authorised to use Italian equipment, and would the Germans please desist? Rommel, commenting astringently on how careless his Allies had been of the same material up to then, merely remarked, 'I was not to be put off', while Halder dourly noted that 'Africa was a problem of equipment and provisions.'

A phase in the African struggle thus ended, and all future operations would start from fresh premises. British attempts to consolidate Tobruk had proved entirely effective, the build-up of material, supplies and manpower going on night after night despite a harrying by Axis surface and air forces. The anti-aircraft barrage thickened while, at the same time, the garrison's inhabitants dug deeper, wired and mined more thoroughly and acquired a grim resolve to carry the fight, when possible, to the enemy. Rommel raised a shield round the perimeter and on the Egyptian frontier behind which to re-organise his rising strength and re-stock his famished depots. He desired no more major operations just then since, more than once, petrol shortages had practically immobilised his armour.

But at least Rommel and his Germans fought in the knowledge that they were heroes in their Fatherland, the darlings of a Propaganda Ministry which recognised a flamboyant character in a romantic setting when it saw one. And even the Italians could bask in reflected glory – at times cheerfully omitting to mention the German leadership which had restored their old frontier. Wavell's Desert Army, on the other hand, despite its triumphs earlier in the year, now dwelt in the realms of public uncertainty. Perhaps, thought the pundits, the previous victory over the Italians lacked the virtue once accorded to it, and possession of Tobruk, after all, represented no more than another defensive delay – a half-saved Dunkirk. When would a British Army defeat the German Army in open combat?

Mr Churchill asked the same question of General Wavell, who showed no aggressive

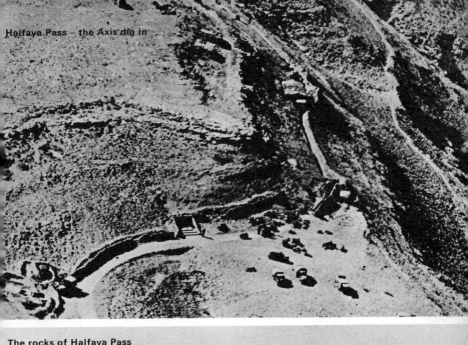

Halfaya Pass — the Axis dig in

The rocks of Halfaya Pass

above: The 88 coming into action below: Dug in below right: Fire! Note the dust and the flank observer looking for fall of shot

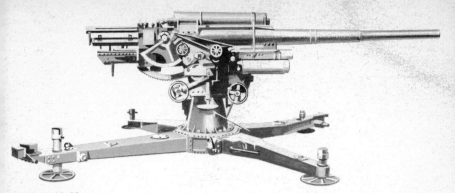

Flak Gun 18-88 mm
Designed as an anti-aircraft gun, the importance of the 88 as an anti-tank weapon was envisaged and practiced long before its appearance with Afrika Korps in the desert. Although it could kill any British tank at long range, its high silhouette and limited protection, linked with restrictions on immediate action, called for the crews to select prepared positions, if possible, prior to action. The 88 was a byword with Allied tank crews throughout the war. To Rommel it was the foundation of his anti-tank capability. Crew: 6. Rate of fire: Up to 20 rounds per minute.

eagerness to put the matter to the test in the immediate future – even though his tank force had recently risen by 238 'Tiger Cubs', as Churchill called them in a moment of parental glow. Indeed, determined that his risk of sending the 'cubs' through the Mediterranean should be justified by instant action, the Prime Minister demanded their participation in a major battle – and Wavell had not the strength of will any

more to deny him, perhaps in view of his knowledge of the Prime Minister's declining confidence in his generalship.

In point of fact, the Germans' military performance outclassed the British in just about every quality except gallantry and perhaps desert experience. In military technique and generalship the Germans stood in a class of their own, their task force combinations of tanks with guns and

Junkers JU 87 – Stuka
right This single engine dive-bomber was standard equipment in the Luftwaffe and gave support to Afrika Korps throughout most of its campaigns. Its highly accurate attacks against British shipping were always an indirect help to the German land forces: on land its impact on morale was not always paralleled by physical damage. As a close support weapon, however, the JU 87 did much to supplement the power of heavy artillery. It was highly vulnerable to enemy fighter aircraft.

infantry rewarding the zeal of their officers by detecting and taking their opportunities without hesitation. In quality and quantity of equipment the advantage in June 1941 rested marginally with the British who fielded 200 against 170 German tanks. The Matilda still outmatched the German Mark IIIs and IVs in all but speed, but the new Crusader tank that came in the 'Tiger' convoy carried no better a gun than Matilda and lost whatever advantage its superior cross-country performance gave, by reason of its depressing unreliability.

Unfortunately for the British, the Germans had learned how to concert the efforts of all arms. The Luftwaffe flew at the request of ground forces and knew how to find and attack targets close to the battle line: anti-tank guns formed screens behind which armour waited to pounce upon any aggressor who might lose his cohesion under the fire of the guns. The Germans fought as homogenous battle groups to a well-founded drill, whereas the British inclined to operate as separate entities of infantry and armour, only achieving mutual co-operation after great deliberation – almost in the nature of an event. By the same token, the closest point to the battlefront at which British air and ground commanders joined their communications lay at Lieutenant-General Beresford-Peirse's XIII Corps HQ – right out of touch with the really intimate detail of the fighting upon which, alone, air power could inject close support for the ground elements. In summary, the Germans were professionals and the British groping their way through amateurism.

Viewed from Rommel's HQ, the evolution of Wavell's attack – Operation 'Battleaxe' – came as no surprise in mid-June. But this in no way made it welcome, since petrol stocks were terribly short and would place an embargo on expansive tactical countermoves. For that reason, Rommel planned his defence with unusual care and precision – but he may also have been wary because of continuing friction with the Commander-in-Chief of the Wehrmacht,

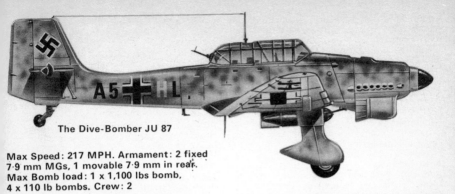

The Dive-Bomber JU 87

Max Speed: 217 MPH. Armament: 2 fixed
7·9 mm MGs, 1 movable 7·9 mm in rear.
Max Bomb load: 1 x 1,100 lbs bomb,
4 x 110 lb bombs. Crew: 2

Brauchitsch, who had complained at the tone of his reports. Halfaya had now been converted into an almost impregnable position, its centre of resistance a battery of 88-mm anti-aircraft guns dug deep into the rocks for use in an anti-tank role, their long barrels just clearing the ground and sweeping the terrain to their front. But this anti-tank screen also extended inland along the Hafid Ridge, making it more difficult for British armour to sweep round to Sidi Azeiz as they had during 'Brevity'. Echeloned back in still greater depth, Italian 'Trento' Division held the area Sollum – Capuzzo – Bardia – all under command of 15th Panzer Division whose 8th Panzer Regiment of two tank battalions (amounting to 80 tanks) lay in reserve between Capuzzo and Bardia. In general reserve, and enjoying a well-earned rest, 5th Light Division waited close to Tobruk.

Air reports and radio intercepts soon indicated the presence of two British divisions in the frontier area, while mounting rail traffic to Matruh and the tenor of radio messages gave ample warning to Rommel of the exact date of the attack – June 15. At 2100 hrs on the 14th he alerted his whole front, and then waited. At dawn three British columns were detected on the march, one along the coast road making as if to climb the escarpment; a second travelling along the top of the escarpment headed for the strongest part of the 88-mm nest, while, out on the desert flank, fast cruiser tanks flung up dense clouds of dust as they probed forward. But there any similarity with 'Brevity' vanished.

Down on the coast the defenders noted with satisfaction that their newly-laid minefields effectively blew the tracks off the advancing Matilda tanks, leaving Indian infantry from 4th Indian Division to tramp forward unprotected into the defending artillery, and then into machine-gun fire as they closed. It was all almost too easy. And on top of the escarpment it proved no more difficult when the Matildas rumbled slowly across the open, the infantry following, but without a round of

artillery fire to fluster the German gunners, for the British supporting battery had become stuck further back in soft sand. Now the 88s made play and ripped the Matildas to pieces, one by one – and the waiting German infantry saw their opposite numbers melt from view – not to appear again.

But on the extreme desert flank the German anti-tank gunners on Hafid Ridge did not have it quite their own way, but, dug into hollows, had to await the charge of fast cruisers from 7th Armoured Division, and dive into slit trenches when nothing could stop them driving through. Here both sides played catch-as-catch-can, the gunners firing as long as they might, lopping off British tanks one by one until the range got too close, while the British, spraying the guns with machine-gun fire (for lack of anything more destructive since their artillery, at first, lay back out of touch) ran wildly in upon them. Hafid Ridge held out all day – the German gunners dying hard by their guns and gaining time for 5th Panzer Regiment to arrive from Tobruk via Sidi Azeiz and intervene during the last hours of daylight.

In the centre of the ridge, too, the German guns fared badly, for here, massed Matildas, supported by infantry and artillery acting in concert after an earlier, unco-ordinated attack had received the same rough treatment as elsewhere, overran the position. To 8th Panzer Regiment trundling down from Bardia in the north to rescue the anti-tank gunners, the sight of burning enemy tanks and the sound of encouraging reports on the air acted like a tonic – with luck they might arrive at the exact psychological moment of enemy disruption – and then they ran slap into real trouble; a complete regiment of Matildas swung around their flank, avoiding the anti-tank gun screen and seized Capuzzo. Horrified at the possibility of Bardia falling to this new threat – and further misled by a gross over-estimate of British tank strength which turned 30 Matildas into 300 (a common enough error amongst those

35

under pressure who are in need of an excuse) 8th Panzer turned tail back towards Bardia.

As dusk fell, Rommel took charge – the British position now clear on his map owing to their generous use of uncoded radio signals. A bold plan crossed his mind. Fifth Light would advance concurrently at dawn with 8th Panzer Regiment, the former in a wide arc to Sidi Suleiman via Sidi Omar, the latter in a shorter wheel round Capuzzo to pin down the main enemy force thereabouts. The genius of this plan resided in the intention to concentrate both divisions '. . . suddenly into one focus and thus deal the enemy an unexpected blow in his most sensitive spot'. Better still, it would catch the British with their armour scattered, while helping to clean up ground that should already have been taken by the German infantry: at best a total envelopment might be accomplished by crushing the exposed enemy against the triumphant defences at Halfaya.

At dawn the drive began, watched from a respectful distance by some wary British armoured cars. The remainder of the British force, at first, went on battering at Sollum and Hafid Ridge – there to become embroiled in a fierce battle with 8th Panzer Regiment as it started south. But this time it was the Germans who found themselves exposed in an unenviable position as targets crossing the open desert at the mercy of British anti-tank and field gunners who had arrived unnoticed during the night. At 0500 hrs, 80 German tanks started the attack: by 1030 only 30 remained fit for action and were back where they started. Much had been done to restore British fortunes.

An altogether different kind of affray broke out when 5th Light Division struck south for Sidi Omar. On this flank the mobile troops of the 7th Armoured Division fought for once as a properly integrated team of tanks and guns, making every possible use of ground by moving at speed into covered positions and then engaging the German column at ranges which they had now learned were the most effective. It needed a cool nerve and clear eye – but there were enough British gunners with these attributes to make it an expensive morning for the Afrika Korps.

Afrika Korps normally chose to develop its tank attacks at a little under 15 mph. Allowing for the fact that the British 25-pounder field guns took about 3 minutes to get on the move after action, this meant they had to limber up in the face of a tank attack when it was still 4,000 yards off or risk being overrun. But the British 2-pounder tank guns were only really effective at 500 yards, not because they could not penetrate, but because accuracy fell off beyond this range, particularly in the dust and shimmer of the desert. Thus, to be sure of a kill, the British tank crews had to wait, nerves-a-tingle, while the German tanks closed in to machine-gun range. But after a few sharp lessons, the Germans tended more and more to stay out of range; in practice, both sides got into the habit of opening fire at 1000 to 1500 yards range – a futile performance since neither were

An Afrika Korps armoured car at rest. Notice the housekeeping arrangements

likely to achieve penetration even if they managed to hit.

So in a series of darts and jabs, the British hung on the flank and tail of 5th Light as it made for Sidi Omar – the desert trail marked by broken vehicles wherever the two sides had actually come to grips. The Spanish Armada struggling up the English Channel must have felt something like 5th Light – and like the Armada, the German formation made port rather battered. Unlike the Armada, however, it was ready for immediate action next day, June 17. Moreover Rommel felt even more certain that his shrewd blow had hit the spot, for the British withdrawal in step with his advance and the persistent wail of complaints on their radio nets concerning shortage of supplies and tank losses, confirmed his superiority. Redoubling his punch, he pulled the remains of 8th Panzer Regiment away from Capuzzo and sent it south and then east, in parallel with 5th Light Division on the 17th, straight for Halfaya.

At first nothing stood to bar his way, for the 7th Armoured Division's cruisers (what remained of them) had pulled back into Egypt to replenish fuel and ammunition, while the Matilda tanks, located with 4th Indian Division near Capuzzo and Halfaya, found the whole enemy armoured force had slipped past them to the south and would soon cut off the retreat of every British soldier west of the frontier. Not waiting for Beresford-Peirse's permission to withdraw, the commanders of 4th Indian and 7th Armoured Divisions ordered their formations back at top speed, hoping that a few Matildas might hold open a passage through which the infantry and guns could escape. Arriving at Beresford-Peirse's HQ a few hours subsequent to this decision, General Wavell thus discovered, to his consternation, that 'Battleaxe' had been blunted without its commander having a say in the act. Rommel and Afrika Korps had been too quick for him.

Scuttling back from Capuzzo and tramping down from the escarpment came the vehicles and infantry of 4th Indian Division, as 15th Panzer and 5th Light Divisions tried to break the tenacious resistance of the handful of Matildas. But once more the tough armour of the British tanks kept them away, and the skill of their junior commanders out-matched that of their German adversaries when the latter lacked support from their 88s. For six hours the opposing forces battled, at times blundering to within almost point blank range, the Germans hanging on to the British flanks, but not threatening to head them off and trap them.

It seems unlikely that Rommel was ever fully aware of this reticence on the part of his panzer regiments, for when they arrived at Halfaya, in the late afternoon, he fondly believed the bulk of the British lay neatly trapped away to the north near Capuzzo instead of safely back in Egypt to the south. Nevertheless, Afrika Korps had scored a decisive victory – its loss of only 25 tanks totally destroyed against 87 British (many only broken down) is only a dram of the full measure.

Tanks in wedge formation

'Battleaxe,' in fact, marked a turning point in the Desert War: indeed it preceded the fundamental turning point of the whole war – the German invasion of Russia on June 22 – by less than a week. But in its more local context Afrika Korps did far more than just defeat another British force – it gave birth to what had always been in gestation, the legend of Rommel's invincibility in the minds of British soldiers, whose convictions were now confirmed when both Wavell, Beresford-Peirse and the commander of the 7th Armoured Division were removed from their posts shortly after the battle. After 'Battleaxe', both British and Germans had a strong respect for the German commander, and while the Afrika Korps hardly felt superior in equipment to the British (their treatment by the Matildas underlined that) it did sense that, in Rommel, it held a trump card, worth more than a division in himself.

War is very much a conflict of psychology and confidence, and the British had now seen two sets of their commanders driven to subservience by one man in a matter of weeks. Those who had fought also knew they had been out-manoeuvred – and some knew why. Yet fresh commanders, coming successively to the fray, did not have time to learn the lesson that mobile war is a game of nerves won by he who understands the risks, together with certain fundamental rules. One of those rules is that, though the relative quality of equipment contains important values, its handling transcends all. Another, that armour must be used concentrated and in conjunction with artillery and anti-tank guns but that, in the desert, infantry on their own are pawns of low price. Fundamentally the British were infantry soldiers who, in 1941, thought and fought in straight lines.

Because he stayed on, Rommel enjoyed the opportunity of teaching the lessons he had learnt to each fresh generation of leaders who arrived to replace the rather high casualties in the higher echelons of his command. He now understood more fully how to combine his tanks with guns, making sure that his anti-tank gun screen should always be well sited as a pivot around which the armour could manoeuvre. He understood far better, too, how inhibiting might be shortage of supplies – though

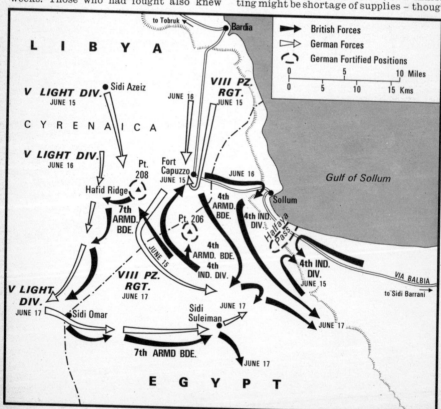

'Battleaxe', Wavell's last desert offensive, comes to grief on the frontier

38

never allowing this to curtail a tactical plan if possible, even when it conditioned his whole basic strategy.

In consequence he thought deeply, if a trifle inaccurately, about the conflicting merits of the British tanks. In this respect he was no expert – very few field commanders could hope to be on so specialised a subject – and vital changes now began to overshadow tank technology. On the eve of the Russian campaign, tanks were on the verge of a rapid upswing in the weight of armour carried and the size of gun mounted. Most British tanks at the outbreak of war were armed with a 2-pounder (40-mm) gun which when it hit, could penetrate the 30-mm armour of the best German Mark III and Mark IV tanks at ranges up to 1000 yards without great difficulty. The German 37-mm or 50-mm guns on Mark III and the short 75-mm on Mark IV were not, however, so effective, as we have seen, against the thick 80-mm armour of Matilda or even the 40-mm of Crusader. But that lesson had been learnt by Rommel in 1940, and a year later more powerful German anti-tank guns began to appear, first on field mountings, and then in the turrets of their tanks. Hence, the long 50-mm on a field mounting started to arrive in the desert shortly after

Battleaxe. Automatically, the range of engagements increased – superior German optical sights facilitating this – and then in March 1942 a phenomenon associated with the thicker German face-hardened armour came to light. At very short ranges the 2-pounder penetrated the German Mark IV with ease, but between 300 and 1200 yards it was found that the shot shattered; then from 1200 yards upwards it would sometimes penetrate again, until it finally failed at 1800 yards. These figures varied with angles of attack and, more so, as armour thicknesses were increased.

Thus, in 1941, the Germans began to forge ahead in technology, while the British almost stood still because, after Dunkirk, all development of new weapons was suspended to allow industry to concentrate on making whatever was already in production, to replace the wholesale losses in France. This qualitative gap was never closed, and bedevilled British armoured formations – and therefore the entire Army – for the rest of the desert war. In so doing it helped restore confidence to Afrika Korps' tank crews whose morale had been noticeably dented during 'Battleaxe'. But in the next desert battle the reticence of the German armour to seek battle with its British counterpart was to be a critical factor.

The penalty of defeat – wounded British prisoners

41

Crusader: battle to exhaustion

One Pz Kw III that could not be repaired. A British Stuart drives by while a signaller works on his lines

The summer and autumn months absorbed both Desert Armies in re-organisation. General Auchinleck took over from Wavell and the British Western Desert Force (or XIIIth Corps as it latterly had been) blossomed into Eighth Army under General Cunningham comprising two Corps – XIIIth and XXXth. Great shipments of men and material poured into the Suez Base carried on the long shipping haul round the Cape of Good Hope from Britain and America, and British morale soared at this effusion of good will and full blooded support. No such substantial reinforcement reached Rommel, nor did he feel the slightest encouragement from a High Command whose attentions were rivetted on the vast conflict in Russia, and who had no desire to stir up a wasp's nest in Africa – a territory they never seemed to understand in any case.

Of course, fresh supplies did reach Rommel – some of them quite substantial – and he received promotion too. Fifth Light was upgraded and renamed 21st Panzer Division and a number of special units were regrouped and given the name 90th Light Division – strong in firepower and mobile infantry, but totally lacking in tanks. But Afrika Korps remained basically the same – an Armoured Corps consisting of two Panzer Divisions – with only on occasion other formations brought under its command. Alongside the German formations stood two Italian divisions – armoured 'Ariete' and motorised 'Trieste' in XX Motorised Corps, plus four infantry divisions. But command of the whole Axis desert force, now called Panzer Group Afrika, now rested with Rommel, while Afrika Korps itself passed into the hands of Lieutenant-General Cruewell. At last Rommel could put into official practice what had been done by expediency and impatient diplomacy in the first battles – stationing Afrika Korps companies amongst the Italians to act as 'corsets', with German officers at hand to lead the malleable, often courageous, and not entirely unresponsive Italian soldiery.

There remained, however, a stiff formality about the German organisation which fell short of the requirement when engaged in the sort of free reconnaissance and raiding practiced by Will o' the Wisp British parties, such as the Long Range Desert Group, deep from the desert wastes. Thus, while the British kept Afrika Korps constantly under observation and occasionally under fire in the back areas, German reconnaissance consisted only of a single, heavy handed raid by 21st Panzer Division towards Sofafi in mid-September. There was nothing waspish about this – for the raiding group consisted of tanks, armoured cars, guns and infantry with support from the air, commanded by General von Ravenstein, the Divisional Commander, and accompanied by Rommel in

person. By bad luck they missed the main British dumps in the forward area and had to retire at breakneck speed to Capuzzo, bombed from the air and chased by British mobile forces.

Yet this solitary probe satisfied Rommel that, because no supply dumps had been found, the British were projecting no immediate offensive operations against him. So, in a state of false security, he turned again to Tobruk, strengthening meanwhile, the fortifications at Halfaya yet further. Nevertheless, he was still fearful that, in the end, the build-up of British forces in the desert might eventually overwhelm him by sheer weight; worried by persistent bombing of his lines of supply and anxious that Italian shipping might fail even to maintain, let alone increase, his own strength, Rommel argued hotly for permission to attack – and at last won his point. Tobruk would be stormed at the end of November by two Italian divisions, plus 90th Light and 15th Panzer, while the remainder of Panzer Group stood on guard against British intervention from Egypt.

But General Auchinleck forestalled him – indeed the British preparations to relieve Tobruk, while its garrison broke out, had been well advanced at the time of the Sofafi raid in September. There is, however, a tribute to Afrika Korps implicit in the very aim and substance of Auchinleck's plan and Cunningham's execution of it. For XXXth Corps, the main British armoured force, was to circle through the desert from the south, with the task of seeking and destroying the German armour, leaving XIIIth Corps to isolate the Halfaya/Sollum area and drive ponderously, with infantry and heavy tanks, to join the central battle near Tobruk. Thus Afrika Korps became the focus of British attention, acting unconsciously in collusion by staying fully concentrated most of the time, while the British, acting in the manner of beaters, spread across the desert in three separate groups.

Because armoured forces dominated in the desert, even when anti-tank guns subdued opposing tanks and caused more casualties than when tank fought tank, the presence of armoured forces assumed similar importance in the desert to the existence of a naval fleet in port or at sea. It followed that the aim of an armoured battle could depend upon the ability of the contenders to preserve their armour in being, and so in this respect, the maintenance, recovery and repair of broken down machines assumed prime importance. Unlike victory at sea when the defeated would have been sunk without trace, victory on land left the battlefield in possession of the victors endowing them with the option of recovering their own broken equipment and demolishing or dragging away that of the enemy. This assumed a hitherto un-

Pz Kw III with L/60 50 mm gun
Along with Pz Kw IV, this tank comprised the main armoured striking power of Afrika Korps. Starting life with a 37 mm gun, it received successive improvements of which the version depicted here was the ultimate in Afrika Korps service. The L/60 gun achieved velocities up to 3,930 feet per second using a special rigid shot that enabled it to engage most British tanks with success beyond 1,000 yards range.
Weight: 20 tons. Speed: 25 MPH. Armour (max): 60 mm. Crew: 5. Armament: 1 x 50 mm gun, 2 x 7·9 mm mg

known significance at this time, for since losses by breakdown were as much the cause of declining tank strengths as destruction by enemy action, occupation of the battlefield immediately after action by the recovery services became a tactical bull point. And in this sort of activity the Germans were superior to the British.

Moreover, in the desert, unmotorised infantry became prey to the smallest band of marauding tanks – so believing wholeheartedly in the traditional omnipotence of infantry, the British were forced to attach a quarter of their 756 tanks (mostly Matildas and Valentines) to the infantry-heavy XIIIth Corps to afford it protection, while the remainder formed the three hunting, cruiser-equipped armoured brigades. Thus British armour fought in four packets, each, to begin with, a little over 150 strong.

The Italian 'Ariete' division had nearly 150 M 13s - poor, obsolescent vehicles, but Afrika Korps was 249 tanks strong, of which 174 were the more powerful Mark IIIs and IVs. The Panzer Group concentrated and backed by its newly arrived, long 50-mm field mounted anti-tank guns, could thus achieve local superiority over any individual British armoured group - though Afrika Korps had no material reserves, whereas the British held a 50% reserve of tanks which could reinforce the front at 40 a day. Therefore, if Afrika Korps, aided by 'Ariete', could achieve a series of fully decisive concentrations against each British armoured brigade in turn, in the

shortest possible time, the British might be totally destroyed before their preponderance in material overwhelmed the dwindling Axis formations.

Stripped to its barest essentials, modern mechanised warfare can have one or two aims, merging into one grand design if knowledge and imagination combine at the apex of command. There can be a battle of attrition, man taking man, machine breaking machine, until only the strongest survives to survey a field littered with wreckage - or there can be a stroke to the brain or heart which paralyses all further action. The theorists yearn for the latter - pragmatists lean to the former, but accept as a bonus anything that might be won by a psychological stroke.

A combination of the two reaches towards the real art of war - sometimes a vision emanating from a single brain, sometimes an evolutionary process procured through the interaction of two or more intellects; Rommel's experience and instincts tilted him towards the practice of shock treatment designed to paralyse the enemy by the insinuation of a psychological embrace: General Cruewell, imbued with the need to destroy to win, strove for material victory. They formed a formidable combination.

A British curtain raiser to their Operation 'Crusader', however, attempted a true stroke at the brain - right, in fact, at the temple - plotting no less than the destruction of Rommel himself. On the night of

Prepared for the worst. Italians M.13's heavily sandbagged to compensate for their inferior armour

November 17, a raiding party which had landed on the coast from submarines three nights before, launched its attack on the house at Beda Littoria which housed the rear, administrative headquarters of Panzer Group, in the hope of killing Rommel on the eve of the main offensive. Simultaneously, other raiding parties infiltrated from the desert in an effort to destroy Axis supplies and aircraft on their landing fields. But while the raids against material achieved some limited success, the attempt of Rommel's life failed altogether, for the subject had flown to Rome for a conference and had not yet returned – and even then Beda Littoria would not have been his destination.

The same night the British main forces approached the frontier in strength, their movements unlike 'Battleaxe', defeating every attempt at discovery – not just because heavy rain grounded Axis aircraft on the eve of the offensive, but also because earlier Axis reconnaissance had utterly failed to detect the well camouflaged dumps and troop concentrations. For this reason little of excitement happened on November 18 : the British armoured brigades spread out like a blind man's fingers from Bir el Gubi to Sidi Omar, their general direction towards Tobruk, senses acute for touch with the Afrika Korps: but Afrika Korps lay hidden between Gambut and Sidi Azeiz and did nothing – simply because Panzer Group did not know until late in the afternoon that an offensive had begun!

Rommel at once called off the projected assault on Tobruk and turned to deal with Cunningham, telling Afrika Korps to launch a reconnaissance in force against the British advancing towards Gabr Saleh, while everything stood fast to await the disclosure of the general shaping of events. This instinct to take offensive action proved fortuitous, for when Colonel Stephan's Battle Group, out of 21st Panzer, struck 4th British Armoured Brigade – the right finger of the British assault – it placed that formation in a dilemma, for not only did 4th Armoured give right flank protection to XXXth Corps in its advance to Tobruk, it also protected the left flank of XIII's New Zealand infantry waiting the order to pass round Sidi Omar.

From that moment, the Germans got on top, encouraged by the Ariete Division holding ground at Bir el Gubi on the 19th, against 22nd Armoured Brigade. Only the centre British brigade, the 7th, won clear to reach Sidi Rezegh – close to Tobruk, badly isolated but poised to make contact with the garrison.

To Cruewell at HQ Afrika Korps the situation in the vicinity of Sidi Azeiz gave cause for concern on the 19th. Fast British Stuart tanks had roared across the Trigh Capuzzo and caught 3rd Reconnaissance Battalion – its commander calling out loud for help, impressing Cruewell with the notion that the British were in strength to the east. As a result, on the 20th he set the whole of Afrika Korps in motion to the *east*, away from the hub of action, thereby eventually marooning it, petrol tanks dry, by mid-afternoon. Lack of accurate and timely information had thus handicapped the Afrika Korps and, worse, split it, because only enough petrol for 15th Panzer

45

A pause in 'Crusader' as prisoners are gathered

could be collected at once.

Taking advantage of this replenishment, 15th Panzer rushed off to the south-west and this time struck lucky – the left flank, in fact, of 4th Armoured Brigade as it gingerly felt its way northwards in search of Afrika Korps. Carving their way through the British formation, the German tank gunners, aided by the setting sun at their backs, shot brilliantly and undoubtedly won this round. Many burning Stuarts lit the evening sky (German losses were only seven tanks) and so far the British armoured brigades had failed, in a singular manner, to come to each others aid.

Moreover Rommel at last knew, on the night of the 20th, where the principal British components of the attack were – menacing Bir el Gubi, facing 90th Light Division as it dug in on Sidi Rezegh to block the approach to Tobruk, while a third component, with its knuckles rapped, halted near Gabr Saleh. By dawn on the 21st, Afrika Korps had combined again – with orders from Rommel to attack north-westwards against the rear of 7th Armoured Brigade at Sidi Rezegh. Thus a sort of military double-decker sandwich formed – Afrika Korps piled on top of 7th Armoured, who piled onto 90th Light, who, with Italian garnishing, pressed down on the Tobruk garrison who, that morning, began to break out. The British 4th and 22nd Armoured Brigades might themselves have squashed Afrika Korps flat against 7th Armoured Brigade – but they held back until, sent forward at last, they found a vicious screen of 88s and 50s ambushing their path, guarding the tail of Afrika Korps to sap British tank strength in a dune by dune encounter.

Screening Tobruk, 90th Light with the Italians had thus only to hang on, back to back, stall the British sortie through the perimeter wire and mines, blunt 7th Armoured Brigade and the 7th Support Group as they launched their prepared assault, and wait to sweep up the survivors once Afrika Korps had descended upon the British to their front. To the Germans' delight the mass of British armour caught between Afrika Korps and 90th Light suddenly seemed to break into three segments. One made straight for Tobruk and into a hail of fire from the anti-tank guns sweeping the face of the escarpment. The second and third segments turned independently towards Afrika Korps and the German tanks, halting as was their method when firing, picked the bones from one segment before the other could close the range. But the third group proved sterner opponents, firing accurately on the move and actually putting elements of Afrika Korps (which was running short of ammunition and fuel) to flight.

Replenishment could now take place at speed since Afrika Korps' northward drive had carried them close to their original base area. By afternoon both Panzer Divisions were back on the rampage, 21st running up against British 7th Support Group and coming under heavy 25-pounder fire, 15th pushing amongst the tanks trying to protect 7th Armoured Brigade's transport. Using their anti-tank guns aggressively in close co-operation with the tanks,

they exacted a heavy toll, breaking off only at the last moment when the tanks of 22nd Armoured Brigade appeared belatedly from the south. Each British armoured brigade had now taken a hammering – 7th had only 28 runners of its original 141 left, but mistakenly sensing success (caused in part by wild, unfounded claims of German tank losses), Cunningham allowed 1st South African Division to move into the armoured melée and sent XIIIth Corps towards Sidi Azeiz – infantry sheep into the wolf's lair – as the preliminary stage of the relief of Tobruk.

Next day, the 22nd, the Tobruk sortie lay where it had stalled on the 21st, half lodged in the Italian siege-lines. Content that his rear held firm, Rommel ordered 'mobile operations' by Afrika Korps south of the Trigh Capuzzo, and Cruewell, planning with deadly skill the previous night, deliberately split his korps, unobtrusively slipping 15th Panzer to the east and leaving 21st Panzer to throw the British off Sidi Rezegh airfield.

Again the British obliged Cruewell. 4th Armoured Brigade failed to make contact; the pathetic remains of 7th Armoured Brigade huddled around 7th Support Group at Sidi Rezegh and blunted itself on a marauding German column; 5th South African Brigade flung itself meanwhile against a German strong-point south west of the airfield and suffered a repulse, while 22nd Armoured Brigade passed unmolested close by to join Support Group at the airfield. The airfield now became a killing ground, 21st Panzer (on Rommel's, not Cruewell's

Rommel assisted by von Mellenthin, pushes his car out of soft sand. General Cruewell – master of the close battle

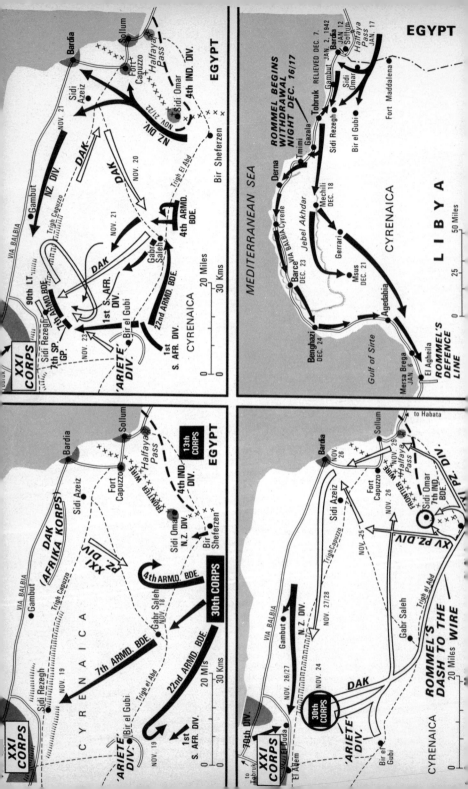

Desert combat:
Space and vehicles

Men and sand

Grenades and close fighting

Charge in the open

left: **Slogging-match for Tobruk: Retreat for the Afrika Korps**

49

Desert Leaguer. Armour and guns outside, soft vehicles inside, sentries on the alert

Tank battle – a British tank burns

The heart of the battle – some vehicles burn while others wait

instructions) charging across it from the west to become involved in a mad whirl of racing vehicles and billowing dust, through which shell fire and fleeting glimpses of vehicles only served to heighten the confusion of a Dantesque inferno. Part of 7th Support Group was overrun, 22nd Armoured Brigade engaged friend and foe alike and took its own share of casualties, while 4th Armoured Brigade held off from a maelstrom it could not penetrate – an appreciation endorsed by the Brigade Commander when he too came under fire from 22nd Armoured Brigade.

Not all of this confusion was apparent to Cruewell, guiding in 15th Panzer quite unobserved from the east. His command thereupon drove straight through HQ 4th Armoured Brigade at last light, illuminated by a welter of flares, capturing the staff, 35 Stuart tanks, a park of lorries and scattering the brigade to the winds. Throughout a night lit by burning vehicles, the battle spluttered and finally guttered out – but Cruewell had pulled aside to give intense thought to what had been achieved and what might be done next. British armour, he thought, must be broken – in fact 7th and 22nd Armoured Brigades possessed no more than 50 tanks between them and 4th had scattered. Obviously the core of surviving British armour lay south of Sidi Rezegh; there too waited 'Ariete' and 'Trieste' divisions and thence he would go with the whole of Afrika Korps' surviving armour and the rest of 15th Panzer, leaving the remains of 21st Panzer to bolster 90th Light guarding the Trigh Capuzzo.

No sooner had the plan taken shape – nothing less than the concentration of every armoured element in Panzer Group in the *rear* of the British – than a long, coded signal from Rommel began to come in. Cruewell could not – indeed would not – wait. At 0530 hrs with HQ Afrika Korps he moved off to place himself at the head of 15th Panzer and then (the first surprise of a shattering day) ran full tilt into the New Zealand Division, advancing westwards south of Trigh Capuzzo. Of the whole party only Cruewell and his Chief of Staff, Colonel Bayerlein, escaped, but the plan went on unaffected. The columns converged inexorably with three armoured divisions and a motorised division descending upon the luckless surviving 7th and 22nd Armoured Brigades, the 5th South African Brigade and 7th Support Group – with 1st South African Brigade coming up fresh, eager and unwary from the south.

Rumbling through the morning mist, Afrika Korps beheld the dream of all tank formation commanders – a mass of unprotected transport in close order. The slaughter began and went on until mounting resistance, hardened by tanks and guns rushing up piecemeal from the south, impelled Cruewell to call a pause in order to swing his punch further to the south. Indeed, it came as a surprise to him to meet the enemy so far south: his blow had struck their flank, not their rear, and prevented the junction with the Italians.

By early afternoon Cruewell's redeployment had taken place. Massed tight, the Germans and Italians trundled north – but the time wasted in linking up with the Italians (whose approach had been tardy) now recoiled upon the Axis force. That morning nothing had stood in the way: now a screen of British anti-tank guns squatted ready, while the vulnerable, soft transport targets had fled eastwards to safety behind Afrika Korps' tail. Instead of rolling at will, shooting up a disorganised rabble, Afrika Korps had now to struggle for each yard forward, every Battle Group fighting an individual action as it ground its way northwards towards Sidi Rezegh through the desperate British. Artillery duels sprang up, guns fired until silenced, tanks halted, blazed away, moved or burst into flames; infantry cowered in their fox-holes and succumbed before the raging armour. And the tank losses mounted in proportion, for Cruewell's attack had ceased to be indirect: now it lunged straight to the mouth of the guns and suffered badly.

This day had been the German 'Totensonntag' – their annual Day of Remembrance for the fallen of the First World War. One of them wrote: 'Dawn came upon the chaos of Sidi Rezegh. Wrecks still smoked. Men lay with glazed eyes staring at a sun that did not rise for them. Lines of prisoners were formed up and marched off' (5th South African Brigade all but ceased to exist) 'escorted by a few vehicles and detachments of our troops. . . . An irrepressible German sergeant-major named Taudt began to sing in derision, "We'll hang out our washing on the Siegfried Line . . .". Some of the leading prisoners . . . glared at him. But the men behind grinned ironically, undaunted. Somebody took up the refrain. In a few seconds the whole column was singing lustily, "We'll hang out our washing on the Siegfried Line . . .". What could we do?'.

Rather – what would they do? Elated in victory but cool in reflection, Cruewell met Rommel near Tobruk early on the 24th and reported the smashing of the enemy at Sidi Rezegh – laced with the warning that some had escaped eastwards. These, he considered, should be pursued to final destruction – the accolade in the classic battle of annihilation that tallied, as in a drill, with Cruewell's superb professionalism. Both he and Rommel were aware that the massed British infantry of XIIIth Corps and the formidable Matilda tanks of 1st British Tank Brigade lay all about Halfaya, strong in Sidi Omar and beyond Sidi Azeiz, making for Tobruk. But the breakout from Tobruk had seized up and

above: Stuka in the dust
German tanks in the dust
right: A ride into battle for Afrika
Korps Infantry

the British force there could be left to the Italians and 90th Light.

But Cruewell's victory on the 23rd had taken place contrary to Rommel's instructions, for if Cruewell had waited for and complied with the long radio message, the result might have been even more conclusive. Forgetting Panzer Group, Rommel imposed his old authority on Afrika Korps, leaping again into the van of the battle, overruling Cruewell's local solution and imposing a seemingly grandiose one of his own.

Afrika Korps would repeat . the decisive counter-sweep of 'Battleaxe' and drive wide through the desert, into the enemy rear, destroying, almost incidentally, the remnants of XXXth Corps, ravaging the plethora of defenceless administrative units spread out *there, succouring the inviolate garrison of Halfaya and Sollum and, above all, severing XIIIth Corps from its base.*

It sounded marvellous and has been hailed as a masterpiece of psychological strategic enterprise; but at once it took the pressure off XXXth Corps, removed the omnipotent Afrika Korps from the point of decision (where it might have recovered its broken down equipment) and saved the British Army from defeat in detail – leaving it free to scavenge the battlefield and repair damaged tanks. Moreover the destruction of yet another British General – Cunningham – made way for the intervention of one greater than he. It seems highly likely that Rommel lost patience: in reasserting his authority he seized a formula that had worked before and put all

to chance, but won a battle of personalities against Eighth Army Commander.

Cunningham's spirit had given way as the news of XXXth Corps' disaster on the 23rd came through. He wished to abandon the offensive – something General Auchinleck refused to accept – and Auchinleck finally signalled his determination to persevere by removing Cunningham on the 26th and replacing him with a stop gap – Major-General Ritchie–a staff officer of somewhat limited higher command experience. This in fact made Auchinleck Rommel's real opponent – a change that only slowly became apparent to Afrika Korps. But as the Korps plunged for Egypt, with Eighth Army's transport scudding across the desert like minnows escaping from a predatory pike, Indian infantry dug in near the

frontier while those working the great dumps paused and wondered if this could be their moment.

Yet again lack of information thwarted Rommel. Two important British supply dumps had been stock-piled and hidden inside Cyrenaica but Rommel did not know they were there and swept blindly past over the horizon, intent on breaching the frontier near Bir Sheferzen. He took with him 21st Panzer, while the rest of Afrika Korps and the XXth Italian Motorised Corps. strung out behind because they had been unable to start as quickly as Rommel wished. Piecemeal they entered Egypt and piecemeal were sent off on separate tasks by Rommel, standing near the frontier like a traffic policeman. 15th Panzer were to destroy the Indians in Sidi Omar; 21st

Panzer were ordered to go to Halfaya – but again Afrika Korps was to fight on its own, for 'Ariete', not for the first or last time, had dragged its feet and then been stopped by 4th Armoured Brigade east of the frontier. And now both Rommel and Cruewell disappeared – the former's car broke down, he was rescued by the latter, then both were lost together in the midst of British units, out of touch by radio with their subordinates.

Complete chaos ensued on the 25th. Fifth Panzer Regiment, instead of accompanying 21st Panzer Division to Halfaya, attacked Sidi Omar unsupported and lost half its tanks to a pair of 25-pounder regiments. Every vehicle was now short of fuel, so 15th Panzer abandoned 5th Panzer Regiment's attack on Sidi Omar and made instead for Sidi Azeiz, while 21st Panzer rushed through Halfaya – cheered on by the besieged – and ran straight into a New Zealand Brigade at Musaid: Ariete still hung back, and so Afrika Korps dwindled rapidly from battle losses and breakdowns.

Meanwhile the British almost flourished. South of Sidi Rezegh XXXth Corps recuperated its strength from battlefield sweepings and reinforcements from base, the New Zealanders struck down the Trigh Capuzzo (past ground where, 48 hours ago, Afrika Korps had stood triumphant), and linked up after a night tank attack, with the Tobruk garrison. Already a wary confidence was returning, justifying Auchinleck's determination to fight on, and his execution of a change in command of Eighth Army on the 26th. Both sides encroached upon exhaustion – but now Afrika Korps, after initial triumph, looked most weary.

With Afrika Korps and 'Ariete' close together at last light on the 26th, the whole course of events again changed. Rommel's attempt at concentration on the frontier had failed, for the place of decision had really remained all the time at Sidi Rezegh, and now Lieutenant-Colonel Westphal, the senior staff officer remaining at HQ Panzer Group, fended off anxious Italian Corps Commanders and braced himself to overrule his chief, Rommel. To him the return of at least part of Afrika Korps to Sidi Rezegh brooked no delay: to that effect he sent a direct order to 21st Panzer to move westwards – and thereby added further confusion to the chaos already reigning around Fort Capuzzo where most of the Korps had gathered.

A good commander persists in his aim – and Rommel persisted with his frontier dream almost to the bitter end – but in the end he relented on November 27, (proving himself a *great* commander), and having done so hurled his armour back into the fray at Sidi Rezegh almost as if the Frontier Raid had never taken place. But during the intervening 72 hours the whole position had reversed. British armour waxed stronger, wiser and more cautious – and though Afrika Korps could, and did, crush New Zealand infantry and reseal the Tobruk perimeter – it now found itself fighting concentrated but with diminished strength and stretched nerves, against an enemy who might make the same old mistakes, but did not do so quite as irrevocably as before.

When Afrika Korps or Italian tanks withdrew, British armour no longer followed as readily as once they did, fearing a screen of anti-tank guns at every crest. Moreover, the Germans began to sense a continuous and perhaps fatal draining away of strength. For instance, they repeatedly hammered the New Zealanders – so hard, in fact, that the Division had to be withdrawn as too weak for battle – but each combat incurred its batch of German casualties, and nothing better than repaired equipment and the scrapings of reinforcement camps came to replace them. Not a single new German tank had crossed the Mediterranean since 'Crusader' began, and the German soldiers were beginning to realise that their enemy merely absorbed their attacks, rebounding elastically once the pressure relaxed; and their commanders and staff appreciated that the ring of British infantry formations gathering round Halfaya and Bardia, and east and south of Tobruk, might soon be impregnable.

The symbols depicting Afrika Korps on the map ceased to represent strength: the defensive line already dug by the Italians back at Gazala began to look most attractive, if only the battle could be broken off.

Heavy in heart, Rommel made one last effort to escort supplies to Bardia on December 3 and 4 – and failed. British bombers covered the battle zone and struck the ports behind; British armoured cars patrolled and raided almost with impunity. On December 4 Rommel's order went out to give up the eastern face of the Tobruk perimeter – the sort of manoeuvre which can give rise to confusion in peacetime exercises and which, under pressure in war, is fraught with peril, needs room and time for safe execution and, in success, is the supreme test of a formation's skill.

Afrika Korps won, striking the Indian troops closing in from Bir el Gubi towards El Adem on the 5th after the Italians had fought a notably stubborn defensive action, and the crisis passed. A clean break had been accomplished, allowing Afrika Korps – just 50 tanks strong – to fall back to cover the southern flank of the Gazala Line while 90th Light withdrew still further to Agedabia – a sure sign that Gazala would not be the last stop, even though Rommel declared it might be.

These were days of immense confusion in German minds – in Berlin just as much as in Cyrenaica. What had once seemed a run-away victory in Russia now hung in suspense, and although the newspaper reports suggested that success must be imminent, Moscow and Leningrad held out and the Russians fought harder. Then from the Pacific came news of the Japanese attack and the crushing blows against Anglo-American sea-power – but what would the entry of America do to swing the scales against Germany? Now in Africa the Axis turned to run and those in the know said there was friction between the Italians, who could not bear to give up Cyrenaica once again – and the Germans who had been instrumental in regaining the country for them. Characteristically, Rommel resisted intense pressure to force him into staying at Gazala, regardless of the reduced strength of Afrika Korps, and of a sharp decline in the fighting power of the Italians.

On December 15 Field-Marshal Kesselring (recently appointed German C-in-C South), the Italians and Rommel faced each other in recrimination around the conference table. Ever since the British had raised the siege of Tobruk, the Italians had endeavoured to frustrate Rommel's intention to depart entirely from Cyrenaica, and day by day Rommel had diplomatically played off British intentions against Italian unreality. Determined to retain power of decision in his own hands, Rommel indicated his intention to hold successive positions – notably those at Gazala – but always with the proviso that if the British drove deep towards Mechili, he would have to retire. He insisted that Tripolitania must and could be held, pleaded for reinforcements in men and material and slyly suggested the Italians might care to return to Tripoli to make the arrangements, while he fought the battle.

The same day, December 15, the British struck the Italians at Gazala, wheeling 4th Armoured Brigade sharply round the southern flank and coming so close to the rear of Afrika Korps as it intervened to restore Italian fortunes, that the British presence passed unnoticed. But other, less important, British movement on the desert flank, gave Rommel his excuse: retirement to Agedabia started and Afrika Korps moved in haste.

By contrast, the resultant British pursuit started slowly and bore the mark of astonishment upon its execution – for a tough resistance had been expected at Gazala. Not until Christmas Day did British forward units reach Benghazi and by then Afrika Korps was safe behind protective lines further south. German stores burned in Benghazi dockyard – but six days previously a freighter had unloaded 22 new tanks for 15th Panzer, while still more arrived at Tripoli. Others unhappily lay at the bottom of the sea – but the overall position might have been worse. Resus-citated, Cruewell struck back hard at the pursuing British. An infantry attack against Agedabia on December 26 was repulsed and then Cruewell sent in a sudden riposte with 60 tanks that destroyed 37 of 22nd Armoured Brigade's machines for only seven German.

Again, three days later, Afrika Korps repeated the lesson in opportunism, striking forward and trading seven tanks in exchange for 23 British and reducing the British armour to impotence. Free to rebuild his strength in peace, Rommel returned to the narrows at Mersa Brega – and there, on New Year's Eve, contrary to instructions demanding the conservation of ammunition, the Afrika Korps loosed off a *feu de joie* of tracer and flares, that drew a counter display from the British watching from a distance.

The honours had come out fairly even and the soldiers had fought each other as men of honour. For the moment, Rommel's chief regrets centred upon the deserted garrisons far off at Bardia and Halfaya, for Afrika Korps could do nothing for them: their final surrender on January 12, 1942 represented a foregone conclusion – the final fruits of British victory.

At this juncture the morale of Afrika Korps might have set at its lowest, but this sort of reaction seems hardly ever to have appeared. A German officer wrote: 'The Afrika Korps for the moment was a beaten force, but not dispirited. I saw no signs of wilting morale among our rearguard troops. We stood and fought wherever there was high ground.'

How could this be? A multitude of factors helped bolster them up – superb training, a proven battle-drill, good reliable equipment, first class leadership from top to bottom, a belief in their cause, a staunch pride in being outnumbered but successful in most combats and, perhaps, a still fiercer pride in their determination to demonstrate a complete superiority over an ally they despised (and who liked them still less). Not for Afrika Korps the chance to reflect on the reason for its defeat. Whereas the British enjoyed sufficient manpower to enable fairly frequent reliefs of men at the front, the Germans fought on and on sending each reinforcement straight into the line, there to stay.

So the Germans, who thought they had lost 'Crusader' because of lack of air support, lack of supplies, lack of information, lack of help from Germany or from the Italians, hardly felt the cold breath of failure at this moment. Few then, and not so many even now, asked if Rommel's dash to the frontier, with its cession of vital ground to enemy forces at the critical moment, lay at the root of the failure. Yet, brilliant as had been Rommel and Cruewell's handling of Afrika Korps in knitting every element of Panzer Group together, they had in the

Alert — 88 crew in action

heat of intense manoeuvring, lost sight of the fundamental aim which must control each and every one of their campaigns; time and material were *not* on their side and only overwhelming victory in a short space of time, could ever bring about an ultimate decision in favour of the Axis in North Africa.

The rate of fire of the 88 depended as much on the skill of the loaders as anything else

Counter-blast to Gazala

When on January 12, the German garrison at Halfaya Pass surrendered, Major Friedrick von Mellenthin, the intelligence staff officer at HQ Panzer Group, presented his assessment of the relative strengths of the forces opposed to Rommel. Once again the British had freely and openly discussed their individual identities and locations on the radio, so the Major's job had not been difficult. In the forward area the freshly arrived and inexperienced British 1st Armoured Division leaned against the German positions at Mersa Brega, its infantry element doubled by the veteran 201st Guards Brigade (whose presence had eluded Mellenthin's scrutiny), its 2nd Armoured Brigade sited in depth near Antelat. 4th Indian Division had been identified in the vicinity of Benghazi – and clearly the British supply arrangements were working at full stretch, for the port lay in ruins (due to German thoroughness) and the long haul from Derna and Tobruk swallowed transport. Moreover, activity by the Royal Air Force had declined – and this, too, seemed to betoken supply difficulties.

Afrika Korps, on the other hand, had redoubled its strength. Thanks to the safe passage of convoys into Tripoli, German tank strength rose to 84 and the Italians to 89, petrol and ammunition flowed again and over 300 German and Italian aircraft could be made serviceable at any one time. Now therefore, was the time – while Panzer Group enjoyed a temporary advantage – to strike a pre-emptive blow to eliminate the threat to Tripolitania. Once satisfied that his transport resources met the likely demands, Rommel sanctioned the raid – but carefully omitted to tell either his Italian colleagues or the German High Command, withholding the plan even from Afrika Korps until five days before its start on January 21.

Two German columns set out from Mersa Brega on the night of January 20 – one, Group Marcks, consisting of 90th Light and part of 21st Panzer travelling along the coast road: the other, Afrika Korps, detouring round the desert flank along the Wadi Faregh. The British fell back with Group Marcks in close attendance, but Afrika Korps stuck in soft sand. Reinforcing success, Rommel at once spurred on Marcks, switching his centre of gravity with light forces in order to keep the British on the run, in the hope that Afrika Korps might catch up in time to support his bold but risky penetration. But the risk was less than it looked.

Creeping up, unobserved, on thirty British tanks on January 22, Lieutenant Schmidt brought his 50-mm anti-tank guns into action. 'The enemy was totally surprised when we opened fire and a dozen Panzers raced down against the tanks . . . With our twelve anti-tank guns we leap-frogged from one vantage-point to another, while our Panzers, stationary and hull-down if possible, provided protective fire. Then we would establish ourselves to give them protective fire while they swept on again . . . He (the enemy) steadily sustained losses . . . We could not help feeling that we were not then up against the tough and experienced opponents who had harried us so

61

hard on the Trigh Capuzzo.'

This inherent weakness evaded the comprehension of the inexperienced Commander of Eighth Army, Lieutenant-General Ritchie, who visualised Rommel putting out his neck to give ' a God-sent opportunity to hit him really hard', despite the fact that 1st Armoured Division lay in the process of annihilation by Afrika Korps. By mid-afternoon on January 22, Marcks had infiltrated amongst the bewildered British at Antelat, wreaking havoc amongst the supply echelons of 1st Armoured Division, until at last light 15th Panzer caught up to join Afrika Korps, once more, for the task of exploiting unexpected success.

Characteristically, on January 23, HQ Panzerarmee Afrika, which had been upgraded to this status only the day before, seethed with dissension on the edge of victory. General Cavallero, the Chief of Staff Italian Armed Forces, had paid a visit to forbid any further advance despite the obvious success, just as he had forbidden any further retreat on the brink of disaster at Gazala six weeks previously. Furthermore, he backed up his demand by ordering the XXth Italian Corps to stay behind at Mersa Brega – telling Rommel, 'Make it no

more than a sortie and then come back'. But Rommel would have none of it, even though his petrol supplies had again fallen low: he would keep at the enemy just as long as they lasted, swing *south* from Antelat through Saunnu, encircle 1st Armoured Division, and then recapture Benghazi. To a German officer complaining of petrol shortage he merely retorted: 'Well go and get it from the British' – a remark in the style of all the best mobile commanders from time immemorial.

Unhappily for Rommel, the very move designed to bottle the British armour removed a stopper from elsewhere. But the armoured battle which developed, when the British 2nd Armoured Brigade delivered a counter-attack, compensated for the omission, even though, for once, lack of mutual assistance distinguished Afrika Korps' performance. Twenty-first Panzer, struck by the first British assault, cried at once for help from the stronger 15th Panzer. But 15th Panzer had another task which HQ Afrika Korps declined to cancel, having experienced 21st Panzer's alarmist calls in the past! Across the plain between Antelat and Saunnu the action intensified, with losses on both sides, though none of a catastrophic nature. In the minds of the

On watch – the tank tracks point to the enemy

Traffic direction. Panzer Divisions could succeed or fail dependent on the efficiency of traffic control
below: Observation. Survival could be resolved by he who saw the enemy first

Petrol – seen here being filled into Jerricans but never in sufficient quantities

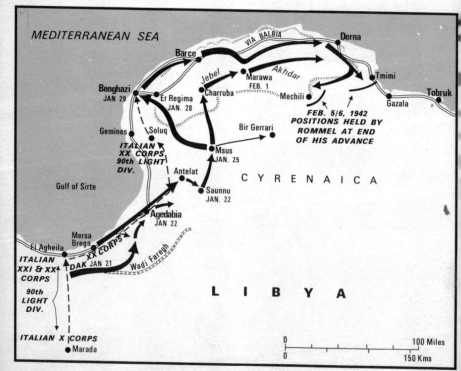

Second time through: Rommel hustles 8th Army back to the Gazala Line

British leaders, however, doubts began to accumulate: the enemy seemed horribly strong, while their own armour wilted, and once that had disappeared the position at Benghazi would become untenable. Plans to withdraw to Mechili were discussed, though Ritchie still considered Afrika Korps had reached its limit (it nearly had) and he determined to hold on at Msus then, since no further advance took place on the 24th (simply because Afrika Korps lay watching an empty pocket that it thought it had sown up south of Antelat). A modicum of confidence returned.

On January 25 the front exploded again. Afrika Korps, grinding north with 15th Panzer, crashed into 1st Armoured Division and reduced it to utter confusion until, like a clockwork tiger run down, the German's 15 mph charge stopped at Msus for lack of petrol. On a reduced scale, Rommel had reached the same stage as on the night of 'Totensonntag'. The British armour lay weakened and scattered, their infantry waited ripe for annihilation, and the British command only belatedly grasped the significance of their speedy collapse. Ritchie still spoke of offensive action when less than forty tanks remained, and aimed to hold Benghazi, still in the belief that his mobile forces could dominate the desert flank. But Benghazi could never be another Tobruk even had a proper defensive perimeter ever been started. However, even Rommel could do very little until additional supplies had been dragged up and the newly conquered battlefield combed for the booty that

would sustain his next move by restoring Afrika Korps' mobility.

Plugged into the most fruitful British radio conversation, von Mellenthin's Intercept Service read confusion in the British chain of command. Clearly they expected Afrika Korps to race eastward along the traditional approach to Mechili. Let them think it, and let Afrika Korps simulate it. Instead Marcks Group was to strike west across country from Msus to cut the roads leading east and north east from Benghazi, while 90th Light advanced from Beda Fomm alongside XXth Italian Corps, (released at last for the pursuit) – the whole deception a superb example of the indirect approach. Rommel was given all the time in the world for, as in the manner of a staff officer who is no great commander, Ritchie continued the debate with his subordinates in a search for the right moment to counter-attack, almost as if engaged in a Staff College exercise. By January 29 he had still failed to reach a decision, but by then Group Marcks had arrived almost unannounced on the high ground overlooking the port after an incredibly skilful night's marching in pelting rain. With 1st Armoured Division (what little remained of it) thoroughly deceived by Rommel's feint and pursuing a wild goose chase hunting a non-existent Afrika Korps towards Mechili, and 7th Indian Infantry Brigade trapped in Benghazi, all thought of offensive action evaporated.

Rommel joined Marcks Group on the last stage of its epic march. To the south, XXth Corps and 90th Light made slower progress against tougher opposition but, when night fell, Rommel felt certain of another triumph, in the light of the perennial glow of burning stores in the battered town ahead. Vile weather had aided his unseen approach and grounded those few of the enemy air force who could reach out from bases behind Derna to hinder and discover him. But the same weather conditions now helped the 7th Indian Brigade in Benghazi. That night the territory south east of Benghazi buzzed with activity where the Brigade, moving in three columns over 400 strong, retraced the course that had been taken by Marcks Group, passed tumultuously through the rearward areas of that Group and XXth Italian Corps, sweeping up prisoners in its path. This exploit seemed worthy of Afrika Korps itself – it certainly took much gilt from the Axis victory.

Next day Rommel entered Benghazi, a signal in his pocket from Mussolini giving authority to begin the advance that had just ended, followed almost immediately by a second cable promoting him to Colonel-General. His stock rose high, his name a symbol of hope in Germany to counter the rebuffs inflicted by the Russians as they flung the Wehrmacht back from Moscow. Now Rommel would have liked to gain more and strike further east, but with fuel resources barely adequate for the journey, let alone a battle en-route, even he could not contemplate this. He could only probe – a maddening business since in material, his losses had been light and the men stood fresh and full of renewed confidence in him. Moreover, not least amongst his admirers, Rommel could now count the soldiers of Eighth Army who recognised in him the sort of genius they were sadly missing amongst their own leaders. Even Mr Churchill helped consolidate his image, referring to Rommel as 'a great General' – partially as an excuse but perhaps also with a hint of wistfulness mixed with the fulsome praise.

Indeed, Churchill showed greater admiration of Rommel than did either Mussolini or his generals. The latter badgered him incessantly, warning him not to go too far, telling him that oil supplies had run out and that their policy rested upon the defence of Tripolitania and that alone. Absence of direction from Berlin bedevilled Rommel now as it always had, for Hitler's strategy omitted the

African shore, while his eyes fixed on Russia and, soon, the Caucasian oilfields. To minds working in both Berlin and Rome that winter, the Middle East itself seemed all too remote. Thoughts of combining a move through the Caucasus with a drive past Suez to Iraq had once tantalised Axis imaginations, but pro-Axis coups in Syria, Iraq and Persia had been laboriously suppressed by the British and Russians during the previous summer. Now in 1942, Field-Marshal Kesselring, responsible mainly for supply in the Mediterranean area, could do little to influence Axis plans when they did not encompass the European vista.

Nevertheless, Kesselring held the key to Afrika Korps' future – control of supplies – and it was to him that Rommel must accommodate himself. Kesselring could initiate or veto operations (such as the elimination of the British offensive base at Malta) that could strengthen or weaken Rommel's hand.

On January 30 Ritchie ordered Eighth Army to fall back to a line at Gazala covering Tobruk, and Rommel willingly followed, dragging the unhappy Italians behind him. In the absence of an offensive Axis strategy in North Africa, Rommel would create his own – by fair means or foul. He realised that the British were pouring material into Egypt, joined now by a flood of American production. Every so often a pre-emptive strike, such as that which he had just executed, had to be made simply in order to stabilise his position. But this state of affairs could not go on indefinitely, particularly since British tactics must improve and they might, one day, find a General who could master him. After all, Afrika Korps could not operate on a shoestring for ever: the wastage of its senior commanders in battle alone illustrated its peril for, of the originals, only Rommel survived, while each Panzer Division had used up two.

Benghazi again. More battered than before but the cinema still works

The strategy of self-help

The year 1942 was to be one of changing fortune when Axis power would pass its peak as a consequence of a year of battle-field attrition.

To the credit of the Axis leaders – Germans, Italians and Japanese alike – their early campaigns had carefully avoided head-on assaults. Nearly every attack had been aimed at the brain rather than the hard muscle of nations such as Poland and France – and more often than not achieved their object by inflicting paralysis. By the end of 1941, however, all three Axis powers had come up against the tough cranium protecting the vitality of America, Russia and Britain. This they could not penetrate and so, in future, their blows lost potency, and their aim became to hold what they had won rather than start new conquests.

But there was one vital strategic target that looked attainable without enormous bloodshed – the Caucasian and Middle East oil complex. Thus, while the Japanese took over most of the Far Eastern fields, the Axis planned their principal blow in 1942 through the Caucasus into the Russian oilfields, with the thought that later they might strike deeper and engulf the fields in Persia and Iraq. Oddly enough, any thought of linking the Caucasian blow with a simultaneous attack from Cyrenaica through Egypt received little serious attention by the Axis leaders at first.

One chink of light relieved Rommel's gloom during a series of baffling conferences in Berlin and Rome in March 1942. Malta, Hitler agreed, had to be eliminated in order to free the sea-lanes to North Africa from interdiction by British air and sea forces based in the Island. To this end, Kesselring was authorised to project a heavy aerial bombardment against the place (throughout March, April and May) as the preliminary to an air and seaborne landing in June (Operation 'Hercules'). The bombardment was also to cover the transportation of greatly increased supplies to Panzerarmee Afrika to enable them to carry out yet another spoiling attack against the British that should culminate in the capture, at last, of Tobruk (Operation 'Theseus'). But, once that had been accomplished, Hitler announced the advance into Egypt was to stop – for nothing of wide strategic importance was in his mind for that area.

Back in Africa, the core of Rommel's hopes lay, as usual, with his own armoured divisions. He calculated that he must attack before the end of May (and thus before 'Hercules') in order to forestall obvious British offensive preparations, and with 332 German tanks including 242 Mark IIIs, of which 19 were 'Specials' with the long 50-mm gun and thicker armour, and 40 Mark IVs, he felt confident that he could smash the British in four days. Tobruk would then fall and thereafter 'Hercules', safe from interruption by British air forces from Cyrenaica, would swamp Malta. After that he might stampede his masters into permitting a resumption of the drive to Suez.

Unlike Rommel, General Auchinleck had to expend persuasion in damping down the enthusiasm of his masters at home. For Mr Churchill wanted action in haste, contrary to Auchinleck's determination to attack only when every preparation had been made. Nevertheless, the British position that grew up behind thick minefields from Gazala to Bir Hakeim was built as a springboard for the offensive rather than a barrier to keep Rommel at bay. In any case, both British and Axis positions could easily be outflanked inland, and for this reason each secured their forward zones with infantry, stationing their mobile reserves in depth to guard the inland flank.

In several aspects – but not in all – Rommel's Intelligence Staff had interpreted the layout of Eighth Army's dispositions. They were aware of the existence of infantry brigade 'boxes' near the coast and at Bir Hakeim as well as the location of some of the armour: but the full extent of the minefield from Trigh el Abd, the location of several 'boxes' – notably the one in the centre manned by 150th Brigade, – and the position of the 22nd and 32nd Tank Brigades had completely escaped their observation. Moreover, the arrival of 167 new powerful American Grant tanks to help equip 1st and 7th Armoured Divisions was completely unknown to them. As von Mellenthin comments: 'Perhaps, fortunately, we underestimated the British strength, for had we known the full facts even Rommel might have baulked at an attack on such a greatly superior enemy'.

In fact, the relative strengths of the forces disposed in the forward areas were closely balanced. The British had the equivalent of three infantry divisions actually holding well stocked 'boxes'. A fourth division, 2nd South African, held Tobruk, although here the defences had been denuded of much that had made them formidable the year before. Two Army Tank Brigades lay close to the forward infantry boxes, hampered in the employment of their full mobility by the insistence of the immobile infantry that they should not be bereft of close armoured assistance – for the infantry's anti-tank gun was mostly still the out-moded 2-pounder: only a few of the new 6-pounders, the equivalent of the 50-mm, had arrived. Poised in the centre and across the southern flank sat 1st and 7th Armoured Divisions – the former containing only one and not its full establishment of two armoured brigades.

Field Telephone, but in the desert radio was more commonly used

69

Messerschmitt BF. 109 F-1.
Against the sparse P.40 Tomahawks and Hawker Hurricanes of the Allies in North Africa the ME 109 F-1. was supreme in quality and numbers. The Africa Korps was therefore almost free from all but the most pressed air attack.

Hercules and Theseus. Kesselring and Rommel shape the plans of battle

XIIIth Corps had responsibility for the actual line and the coast, while XXXth Corps took care of the mobile troops and Bir Hakeim.

Matching General Ritchie's concentration, Rommel could produce four Italian infantry divisions grouped in two corps, the Xth and XXIst, neatly corseted by selected German infantry, all pressed up against the Gazala Line under General Cruewell – and called 'Group Cruewell'. The decisive mobile arms were XXth Italian Corps, with Ariete Armoured and Trieste Motorised Divisions, and Deutsches Afrika Korps with its two veteran Panzer Divisions and 90th Light attached.

In numerical terms, 90,000 Axis faced 100,000 British: 332 German and 228 Italian tanks opposed 849 British: and in the air 497 serviceable Axis aircraft could outnumber 190 serviceable British aircraft at the front – although both sides might draw on many more from outlying theatres. So, the Germans possessed the edge in the air as well, their Messerschmitt 109 F Fighter outperforming all its rivals. In terms of supply, the British lived in luxury compared with their adversaries and with the passage of every day waxed richer – not least because the railway line from Egypt now stretched forward to Belhamed and reduced reliance on the hazardous sea route to Tobruk; for overall, the Luftwaffe succeeded quite well in hampering both sea and land supply routes. But by locating their supply bases near the front with offensive operations in mind, the British made certain of doubling the need to protect them in the event of a defensive action having to be fought. And by mid-May General Auchinleck realised that Rommel's attack would forestall his own,

Overture to Theseus – the Luftwaffe on its way

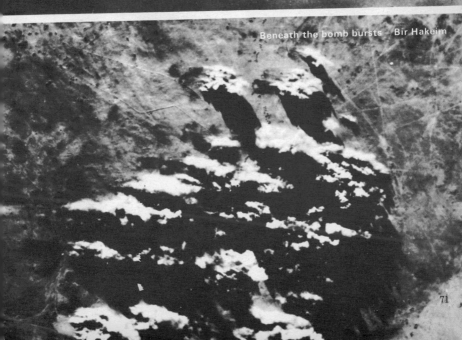

Beneath the bomb bursts – Bir Hakeim

71

Battle group in the advance. Most of its elements such as tanks, towed artillery, armoured infantry and the command elements at the head of the formation are here

Nehring plans a battle with his aides and staff

72

regarding it as likely that the main punch would come in the centre in order to carry straight through to Tobruk. But Ritchie was more inclined to expect it south of Bir Hakeim as part of a wide outflanking wheel. Administrative restrictions in the desert are all embracing – they either encourage a commander to go the longest way round that supplies permit, avoiding as many obstacles as possible in an effort to occupy vital ground in the enemy's rear, or they permit him to hammer at strength with brute force. In the event, Rommel feinted, sending Group Cruewell to demonstrate on the night of May 26 in the centre, but wheeled XXth Italian and Afrika Korps southward as Ritchie expected. Thereafter he intended to move towards Acroma, with Afrika Korps and XXth Corps tasked to destroy the British armour while 90th Light raided the supply bases between El Adem and Belhamed – the whole mass supplied by transport columns for four days – plus whatever could be captured en route.

Fundamentally the success of Rommel's plan depended upon the elimination of the Bir Hakeim box linked with the predictable reaction of British armour. The Free French Brigade holding the box could interrupt the supply line feeding Afrika Korps: thus its early elimination should have assumed high priority, whereas, in fact, Rommel gave the task to XXth Corps in a rather off-hand manner. The British armour was expected to fight in its customary piecemeal fashion, but its deployment rather further south than had been expected came as a surprise, reflecting Ritchie's correct divination of Rommel's plan. Moreover, in writing, (if not later in deed) Ritchie agreed with Auchinleck that the armour must act in unison. So the preliminary British plans by no means permitted Rommel to have it all his own way.

But plans are one thing and their execution another, and something the forthcoming battle never did was keep to

plan: inexorably it grew as an expression of the capability of the Higher Commands to assess and improvise at speed, and the ability of the fighting men to adapt themselves to a succession of unique situations.

Part of XXth Italian Corps – the Trieste Division – got lost and bogged in soft sand on the way to Bir Hakeim during the night of May 26, and 'Ariete' made no impression next morning against the Free French Brigade in the box. Anyway, what little chance Rommel had of achieving surprise evaporated almost as soon as Afrika Korps moved, since they were spotted and shadowed by South African armoured cars throughout the night. Thus Cruewell's overt activity with Italian infantry helped by the loan of panzers from Afrika Korps on the afternoon of the 25th, went for nought. The British were thoroughly warned. Yet to the Germans it quickly became apparent that their opponents had learnt nothing from the past, for at once the same old British mistakes exposed themselves; 3rd Motorised Brigade was overrun in isolation almost at will by 'Ariete' and part of 21st Panzer, and shortly afterwards 4th Armoured Brigade again on its own, lost nearly half its strength against 15th Panzer and, worse, had to quit the battlefield.

Afrika Korps and 90th Light leapt ahead – the latter capturing the commander and staff of 7th Armoured Division, the former taking on 22nd Armoured Brigade when it appeared in isolation, destroying 30 of its tanks. One by one, to Rommel's early delight (but not his surprise) the British formations offered themselves for destruction to his battle groups, while 90th Light laid its hands on some supply dumps in rear. But in the afternoon his elation turned to disquiet as, all of a sudden, nearly three brigades of British armour converged on his columns from both sides, just as they ran into the box manned by 201st Guards Brigade at Knightsbridge. At once the new Grant tanks made their

A present for Rommel. Abandone[d] British 2[5]-pounder field gun

A surprise for Rommel. A knocked out Grant tank

presence felt in a way more pronounced than when they had first been met that morning. Mark IIIs and IVs took hits and burst into flames, while, distressingly, the Grants seemed to defeat hits made in return. The technological balance had swung against Afrika Korps: at once it had need to adjust its tactics.

By nightfall Rommel's position was by no means as happy as once he hoped it would be. Ariete had failed to capture Bir Hakeim; 90th Light lay close to El Adem, isolated and under severe air attacks while 15th Panzer cowered near Knightsbridge immobile for lack of petrol. So, on the 28th, only 21st Panzer could act offensively towards the coast (capturing Commonwealth Keep in rear of the British infantry on the coast) while 'Ariete' skirted Bir Hakeim only to run into British armour before it could link up with Afrika Korps. Meanwhile, 90th Light gave way before 4th Armoured Brigade and ran south and west to escape destruction.

Nobody could blink the fact that, by the morning of the 29th, Rommel's mobile force had utterly failed in its task and now, itself, stood in dire peril – a condition that percolated only slowly to the understanding of Panzerarmee when, by degrees, it discovered that its supply route south of Bir Hakeim had been cut and the British minefield linking that box with the northern front was much thicker than expected. Work began on a short-cut lane through, in complete ignorance of the fact that its far end would be blocked by the whole of the British 150th Brigade, hiding in a box near Sidi Muftah. Thus the passing of supplies to Afrika Korps through this shortened route could not be accomplished until a path had been cleared through the mines and the, as yet undiscovered, 150th Brigade box eliminated.

In the meantime, as British armour closed in, the German casualties and difficulties mounted. Cruewell fell a prisoner, von Vaerst, commander of 15th Panzer, was wounded and several German infantry units were overrun. Supplies, above all petrol and water, ran short – sufficient for the day only arriving because Rommel went back in person to guide the columns: but such a hand-to-mouth existence could not last for long.

Throughout the 29th those Germans who had arrived east of the Gazala Line, drew back to concentrate north and east of the 150th Brigade Box, in a tight defensive perimeter of their own – the Cauldron – while, from the west, Italian divisions in Group Cruewell (temporarily commanded by Kesselring who had arrived on a tour of inspection) commenced the tortuous clearance of lanes in the minefield through which supplies could pass direct to Afrika Korps.

Now began a race against time. Rommel had to clear the lane whilst simultaneously holding off the British armour, and this indeed, at General Ritchie's command, had chances on the 29th, 30th, and even on the 31st, to crush Afrika Korps as it lay in defence. 150th Brigade Box contained 21 days' supplies – although, under pressure of battle, these would be consumed at seven times the estimated rate: nevertheless, the whole weight of the three British armoured brigades lay concentrated close by, part of 1st Tank Brigade had moved into the 'box' and 32nd Tank Brigade was assembling north of the Cauldron, while Ritchie waited for the position to clarify. Meanwhile Rommel's men worked away at the lane through the minefield while their concentration in the Cauldron took shape – until suddenly it dawned on them that the prospective supply lane was dominated by 150th Brigade Box.

This discovery, on the night of the 29th/30th, thoroughly disrupted Rommel's plans. No longer could he project ambitious manoeuvres against the British armour or against Bir Hakeim: sheer survival took first priority.

If Afrika Korps and Rommel expressed surprise at the power of the Grant tanks, it was as nothing compared with their surprise when, with their backs to the mines and 150th Brigade Box, no armoured attack crushed them from north and east. The British commanders were, in fact, thinking deeply about the prize that soon might fall to them – perhaps with hardly a fight if Rommel's supplies became exhausted – but unfortunately for them, all they did was think – for a week – but did not commit a single major attack until June 5.

The trouble was that Command in Eighth Army worked by remote committee, with General Auchinleck in Cairo chairing a long range meeting with Ritchie and his Corps Commanders, while the Divisional Commanders often took enforced action in the absence of co-ordination from above. In Panzerarmee, command found expression in a direct and forcible manner, making use of whatever advice could be obtained, but swift and sure (right or wrong) at the behest of one brain and personality – Erwin Rommel.

Late on the 30th the German Cauldron defences looked quite secure, but the absence of fresh supplies (because 150th Brigade Box still stood in the way) reduced this apparent strength to nought. In answer to a complaint by a British officer on the 31st that the water ration did not meet the needs of the prisoners, Rommel replied: 'You are getting exactly the same ration as the Afrika Korps and myself – half a cup. But I agree we cannot go on like this. If we don't get a convoy through tonight I shall have to ask General Ritchie for terms'. And he set a deadline at mid-day the 1st.

Helped once more towards equality in strength with the enemy when unco-ordinated, local attacks by British infantry and armour had fallen foul of his anti-tank screens defending the lips of the escarpments rimming the Cauldron, Rommel feverishly hammered away at 150th Brigade Box with artillery and dive bombers in preparation for a full-blooded assault early on June 1 – his last chance.

In choking dust, blistering heat and a crescendo of sound, the thirsty British fought back – their senses reeling with desperation and a feeling of isolation, but always in the hope that help would soon come. Unfortunately General Ritchie seemed to be incapable of any action beyond exhorting them to persevere, and throughout the morning infantry and armour tangled bitterly amongst the British positions. By early afternoon all

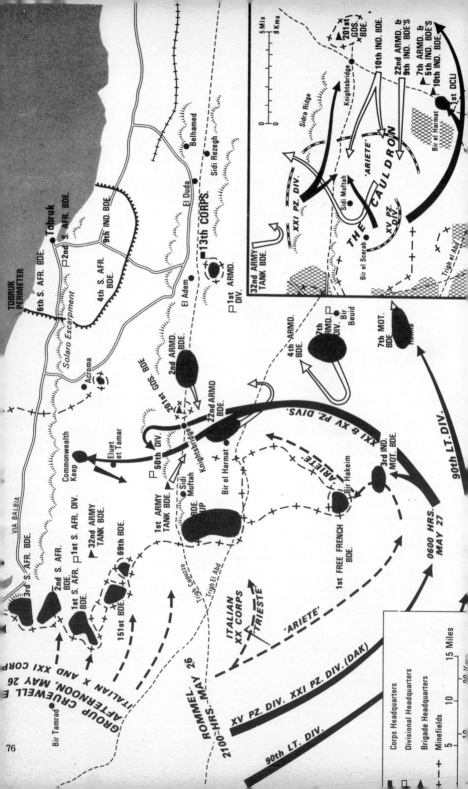

Bombardment: Afrika Korps field artillery takes on the British

was over – Rommel had just beaten his deadline – and it remained simply to bury the dead and evacuate the prisoners. Then, almost as a valedictory salute to their fallen the British launched a feeble relief that night – a total fiasco, interpreted by the Germans as only a reconnaissance, even though intense shell fire wounded Rommel's Chief of Staff, General Gause.

The British fought at Gazala by fits and starts: each major move developing slowly and ponderously, each blow against them prompting a pause for reconsideration which interrupted the continuity and flow which alone creates the inner power of a mobile action. Afrika Korps hardly ever paused (unless it had run out of petrol) and by following a well proven dictum that in armoured warfare one cannot afford to stand still, it kept its opponent in constant uncertainty. So, all the time Afrika Korps recuperated within the Cauldron, it also fought 150th Brigade Box, erected stronger defences for the attack it felt must come from the east, and planned its next offensive stroke – the elimination of Bir Hakeim.

Leaving Afrika Korps and 'Ariete' in the Cauldron, 90th Light and Trieste moved south to deal with the Free French, and the Luftwaffe bombed up for a supreme effort. But although the ten-day bludgeoning of that formidable (but somewhat forlorn) garrison – from June 2 until the 10th, attracted the attention and imagination of the whole front (and later the world), it in no way altered the fact that wherever Afrika Korps lay, *there* brooded the real implement of decision.

In the small hours of June 5, General Ritchie at last launched his attack against the Cauldron, and that day all Panzerarmee and HQ Afrika Korps lay not far apart in the centre of the battle; to the north 21st Panzer held one rim, to the south 15th Panzer the other, being actually engaged in clearing gaps through the minefield through which, next day, it intended to raid the Bir el Harmat area to salvage broken tanks. 'Ariete' held the eastern face of the bowl and it was here that, at 0250 hours on the 5th, a heavy barrage of British artillery fire fell, causing the watchers in the Cauldron anxiously to scan the horizon where it glittered with flashes – a most awe inspiring but utterly wasteful spectacle since, shortly, 'Ariete'

An 88 at night.

reported that the British gunners had engaged empty desert.

Nevertheless, the night assault by Indian infantry that followed the bombardment carried all before it – 'Ariete' gave way and British armour flooded in pursuit, directed right at the centre of the Cauldron – but also into the teeth of a fire by Afrika Korps gunners whose composure had not been disturbed in the least. It was a perfect ambush from which salvation came only from retreat by the attackers. Somewhat astonished by the manner in which, sometimes, the British attacked with barely any attempt at artillery support and, at others, sent in tanks whose activities in no way coincided with operations by infantry, Afrika Korps picked its targets almost unmolested, and by early afternoon still retained full control of the Cauldron, except where the initial penetrations had eaten into its eastern side. One haphazard assault by 32nd Army Tank Brigade on the north rim actually suffered complete repulse with the loss of 60 tanks.

This gave Rommel his chance. Out through the fortuitous gaps in the southern minefield raced 15th Panzer, to sweep round the southern flank, join with units sent from Bir Hakeim, then successively to roll up each and nearly every unit which waited ready to attack the Cauldron from the east. Next 21st Panzer struck eastwards from the Cauldron. Within hours, those British units which had not been destroyed were isolated, their headquarters smashed or dispersed, their ingenuity devoted to escape and self-preservation. And General

Ritchie, it seems, hardly realised what had occurred or what portended.

But Afrika Korps and Rommel knew only too well, particularly when no serious counter-attack by British armour occurred next day. Again, the British had withdrawn to repair their strength, to renew the 'command' debate and deliberate over yet another sterile plan. For the British holding the coast road with their line bent back behind Knightsbridge and with armour in disarray, time stood still. But for the French Brigade in Bir Hakeim (many of whom, incidentally, were Germans who, pre-war, had enlisted in the famous French Foreign Legion), time lost all meaning amidst a welter of bombs, shells and assaults. Up to the British defeat in the Cauldron their fight carried conviction: thereafter it became a matter of national honour, for no help other than defence by fighter aircraft above, could come. Sensing this, Rommel confidently split Afrika Korps, leaving half to watch Ritchie in the north and sending the rest to put more punch into 90th Light and Trieste's unavailing efforts to subjugate the garrison. With Bir Hakeim his, he reasoned, the way towards his original aim of operating freely in the rear of the British line would be half way to completion.

It can be debated that Rommel might have contained Bir Hakeim with light forces, and immediately pressed home the advantage he had won in the Cauldron on the 5th. But there is a subtle difference in his behaviour during this phase of the Gazala battle compared with its earlier part – and indeed to his handling of Afrika Korps at the critical moments in 'Crusader'. On this occasion, he curbed those inclinations for a tear-away lunge, and concentrated, instead, on the meticulous step-by-step destruction of the enemy in detail. He even went so far, as we have seen, to detach tanks from Afrika Korps with a view to using them as part of a deliberate assault with infantry at Bir Hakeim – rather in the same manner as might the British.

In the event only 15th Panzer's infantry took part in the final assault on the French, but the fact that its armour occupied that piece of desert on the night of the 10th/11th, when the French, at their last gasp, received permission from Ritchie to break out, poised Afrika Korps in instant readiness to attempt, once more, what had failed on the first day of the offensive – to break through to the coast. This time, however, Afrika Korps lay more than half-way to its objective, for 21st Panzer and 'Ariete' still held the Cauldron, and their supply lines operated clear of obstructions. Tank strengths had declined, of course, being only 124 in Afrika Korps and 60 in 'Ariete', whilst the infantry had suffered even heavier losses; but morale attained its peak. With the British, whose tank strength on the 12th amounted to only 285, including 83 Grants, the state of morale sank.

Strong in the knowledge that, once again, the British commanders were bickering amongst themselves (their radio still provided an admirable sounding board), Rommel shot out fanwise from Bir Hakeim, the right segment of the fan (90th Light) making south of El Adem, the centre (15th Panzer) towards El Adem, with Trieste filling the gap between 'Ariete' and 21st Panzer, who already projected the left segment around the Cauldron. In theory, the right segment could have been caught and killed in the open desert, for by breaking clear of the intermingled confusion between Bir Hakeim and the Cauldron, the advancing columns exposed themselves to untrammelled attack by the Royal Air Force, who up to then, had been inhibited by the danger of bombing friend as well as foe. They also invited a full blooded and concentrated assault by two of the three British armoured brigades from where they lay close to Knightsbridge.

For the best part of the 11th and 12th while his right flank columns pushed tentatively outwards, Rommel awaited a British counter-attack which never came. 15th Panzer moved up slowly and carefully, bound by bound, from the south, launching only a speculative prod in the direction of Knightsbridge. Satisfied at last that this was no trap, Rommel then sprang up, telling 21st Panzer to break out of the Cauldron and catch the British in rear while their attention focused on 15th Panzer. To the Germans listening to the British radios, it sounded as if the lack of activity stemmed from flat refusals to obey orders to advance. In fact, the reason was almost as bad – simply a typical disagreement amongst commanders (who had acquired an invidious habit of querying orders), one of whom had got lost hurrying on his way to yet another conference. Caught in the void of uncertainty, 22nd and 4th British Armoured Brigades stood footfast, wide open to domination – a fate not long delayed – then to be pitched to the verge of destruction as 22nd Armoured Brigade, rushing south to answer the calls for help from its companions, itself ran into a deluge of accurate fire.

General Ritchie, with justice, might easily have echoed Admiral Beatty's cry at Jutland when his battle cruisers blew up one after the other: 'What's the matter with our bloody ships today?' The answer, in essence, was the same – superior guns and projectiles aimed through better instruments were outclassing a willing and brave foe who had been out-manoeuvred at the vital point. In the air, too, the British failed, losing more aircraft than the Luftwaffe, and achieving less damage with their predominantly high level bombing sorties than the dive bombing of the German Stukas. British tank losses, however, escalated to catastrophic dimensions – no less than 138 vehicles destroyed by noon on the 13th – by which time the Afrika Korps had advanced round the Knightsbridge box, isolating it, and had become established on the Rigel Ridge, threatening a last dash to the coast.

In the midst of a dust storm a highly confused battle billowed on the ridge and round Knightsbridge Box. Here the British flew apart in distress and the Germans coalesced as a unit to grip this key territory. The 'box' had to be evacuated that night, carrying the implication that the intact 'boxes' holding the northern sector of the Gazala Line on the coast could no longer remain occupied. Only 70 British tanks survived and almost every one of those lost had fallen, along with a mass of other material, into Axis hands.

British armour could only look to its own salvation: their infantry had now to do the same, and this Afrika Korps wished to deny them. Already they could see the South Africans pouring back along the coast road to Tobruk (a movement left almost unmolested by the Luftwaffe because it had been called away to bomb a Malta convoy) and they knew that a major break-back must take place that night. But this time, alas, not even Rommel could goad Afrika Korps into action. Von Mellenthin records, without rancour, 'The fact is that the Afrika Korps had reached the end of its tether . . .; it was impossible to rouse the men'. And so the escape of the

South Africans passed unhindered, and a remarkable move *westward*, through the Italians, by 50th British Division, before turning south and doubling back through the desert, lost nothing by its daring success, but evaded exhausted foes who might easily have been overrun themselves that night if and when they had been proved too tired to resist.

In the final analysis, therefore, the total destruction of the British had not been achieved, and to the east they gathered once more, in and around Tobruk. But the essential component in desert warfare – armour – had almost disappeared from the British order of battle at Knightsbridge, and what little that remained lacked cohesion. It had yet to be seen if Rommel's weakened striking force could push the enemy away to the frontier and take Tobruk – if, in fact, Tobruk was to be defended at all. Either way, time could not be lost, for each wasted hour gave the British further opportunities to recover and to destroy stores in the bases Rommel must capture.

**The heart of the Afrika Korps –
a Pz Kw III with its crew**

Tobruk
the fatal bait

Rommel had one over-riding ambition on June 15 – to capture Tobruk. As it happened the British hesitated over their decision to make a fight of it, since the defences lacked the strength of a year ago: a staff officer who asked for the minefield plan, found it hopelessly out of date because many mines had been used to fill the Gazala Line. Nevertheless, a last minute decision to throw in a predominantly infantry garrison of South Africans, Indians and British – short of artillery and with only two weak tank battalions – forced the fight that Rommel expected. And although some strong British desert 'Boxes', supported by armour, impeded his approach to the perimeter on the 15th, he did not hesitate. In every department, above all that of morale, Afrika Korps and the Italians fought as an invincible host, before which the British retreated in confusion to Egypt.

Sweeping south round the perimeter and driving all before them (with further significant tank losses to the British), Afrika Korps completed the investment of Tobruk on the 18th, and 90th Light occupied Bardia next day – putting a wide expanse of desert between the foremost British columns and the isolated port. With the original assault plans of pre-'Crusader' vintage taken out of the files, the staff of HQ Panzerarmee had only to bring them up to date – a task made easy in one sector where the ammunition dumped for the original November operation, was found where it had first been placed. Rommel issued orders for the attack even as the ring closed round Tobruk: the British would be granted neither respite nor warning.

Speed, in fact, was the essence of the plan. There was to be no movement into the assembly areas before the afternoon preceding the attack, reconnaissance and artillery preparation thus being reduced to a fraction of the volume normally to be expected for so important an operation. Bearing in mind that, under the terms of the original plans, the capture of Tobruk would terminate Operation 'Theseus', Rommel's careful husbandry of his armour at this moment betrays his studied intention to continue mobile operations eastwards after Tobruk had fallen. By resisting requests to use armour to help clean up isolated British boxes between Tobruk and Egypt, and by insisting on leading the assault on the perimeter with infantry and engineers supported by a heavy bombardment –mostly from the Luftwaffe – Rommel

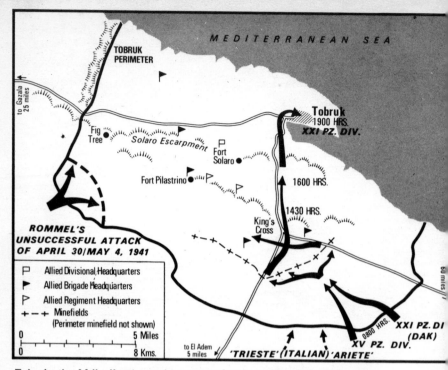

Labels within the map:

MEDITERRANEAN SEA

TOBRUK PERIMETER

to Gazala 25 miles

Fig Tree

Solaro Escarpment

Fort Solaro

Fort Pilastrino

Tobruk
1900 HRS.
XXI PZ. DIV.

1600 HRS.

1430 HRS.

King's Cross

ROMMEL'S UNSUCCESSFUL ATTACK OF APRIL 30/MAY 4, 1941

⌐ Allied Divisional Headquarters
► Allied Brigade Headquarters
▻ Allied Regiment Headquarters
+—+—+ Minefields
(Perimeter minefield not shown)

0 _____ 5 Miles
0 _____ 8 Kms.

to El Adem 5 miles

60 miles

0800 HRS.

'TRIESTE' (ITALIAN) 'ARIETE'

XXI PZ. DI (DAK)

XV PZ. DIV.

Tobruk: the Afrika Korps gets its revenge for the ordeal of the 1941 siege

preserved his tanks for future contingencies.

Kesselring now gave unstinted help, for the Air-Marshal believed that once Tobruk had fallen, 'Hercules' (the attack on Malta) must take place or else the supply situation would be for ever in jeopardy. So every bomber he could muster in North Africa (150 all told) plus a few from Crete, were despatched to the assault, culminating in an aggregate of nearly 600 sorties in one day, most of them aimed at the south-eastern sector of the perimeter. Here the entire weight of Afrika Korps would be launched in depth on a narrow front, at a single Indian infantry battalion – with XXth Italian Corps widening the frontage of the assault against a second British battalion on the left. Linear defences could not resist this treatment.

From the point of view of the defenders, the next 24 hours represented an un-paralleled example of faulty battle drill hitched to a straight forward immobility. Individual British units and the individuals within them fought with desperate courage – but that about summed up British performance which was an unco-ordinated succession of magnificent solo efforts. In the open desert, Afrika Korps had grown used to combating single armoured brigades, and defeating them: at Tobruk they met single batteries and single tank squadrons in solitary succession, so the

outcome never looked in doubt.

No operation of war goes completely according to plan, but the maintenance of momentum within a planned timed framework can be mightily encouraging – and this Afrika Korps experienced from the start. Unhindered as they formed up at night, the infantry crept forward prior to the Luftwaffe's flaying of the frontal British positions at first light. Less than two hours later – at 0700 hours – German engineers had begun filling in the ditch while the infantry, screened by smoke, filtered ahead, dodging from trench to trench, mopping up as they went. When the leading tanks of 15th Panzer crossed the ditch at 0830 hours the signs of victory could be clearly read, for the British response possessed none of the controlled violence of a year ago, and their artillery fire started late and fell wide – a critical deficiency in defence. Thoroughly encouraged, the advance began to quicken, directed from the fore by General Nehring, and halting momentarily only when isolated enemy batteries came into action, or single squadrons of tanks made their solitary contribution. By 1400 hours Afrika Korps dominated the Pilastrino Ridge from whence it could shell the harbour; now, since the last of the British armour had been destroyed, the static garrison lay at the mercy of a pre-eminently mobile foe.

Next day, the 22nd, Afrika Korps enter the defeated fortress

Hardly any of the defenders escaped, or the collapse had been so rapid that no time was left to plan a breakout: the last British troops reluctantly laid down their arms on the morning of the 22nd, although most had done so by the evening of the 1st. To quote an Italian: 'It had all happened so quickly; fortifications, harbour and town, all recaptured in the space of a few hours. The great mass of masonry and twisted metal was still warm and quivering, like an immense body newly slain . . . but the chaos had not prevented the Germans from placing guards over the warehouses . . . There were stacks of tinned beer, huts bursting with pure white flour, cigarettes, tobacco and jam; gallons of whisky; priceless tinned food of all kinds; and tons of khaki clothing . . .'

More important still, as Rommel's staff soon discovered, considerable stocks of water and, above all, vehicles and petrol had escaped demolition and would form the life-blood of whatever Rommel decided to do next – for, naturally, before the last shots had sounded in Tobruk, Rommel worked busily to twist Axis strategy to his way of thinking. Full of congratulation and proposals to redeploy for 'Hercules', Kesselring flew in to HQ Panzerarmee on the evening of the 21st, to be met by a vibrant Rommel who insisted that the fruits of victory must not be wasted – there could be no time to await the capture of Malta if an invasion of Egypt were to reach the Suez Canal before the British recovered. Coolly, Kesselring pointed out that without full air support an advance

such as that must fail – and air support had been booked for Malta – which, incidentally, in the absence of the Luftwaffe when it engaged in the land battle, was beginning to act offensively against the sea-lanes again. Von Mellenthin says, '. . . the discussions became exceedingly lively'. The two commanders failed to agree and Rommel despatched a personal liaison officer to put his views to Hitler and signalled Mussolini in similar vein.

Next day Rommel heard he had been promoted a Field-Marshal by Hitler – and celebrated by ordering Afrika Korps towards the Egyptian frontier on the assumption that Hitler would give retrospective permission. He judged well, for Hitler had always felt luke-warm to 'Hercules', fearing that the Italian assault force would fail and demand yet another rescue by the Axis just after a great offensive had been launched against Russia into the Caucasus. On June 23 Rommel entered Egypt, with the full permission of both Dictators, coupled with the decision to postpone 'Hercules' until September. No Rubicon this – in theory he could always pull back if the opposition magnified.

Ahead an astonished British force dug in at Mersa Matruh, back where they had been at the beginning of the Desert War, for their Commander-in-Chief did not believe Rommel had the resources to reach Cairo and appreciated: 'There is no natural position east of Halfaya which enemy could hold successfully against superior forces'. Could he be wrong again – as so often the Afrika Korps had demonstrated?

El Alamein: the straightjacket

In the realms of battlefield tactics, opportunism can be a virtue, but the strategic movement of troops to the battlefield is, by nature, a long-term exercise, demanding foresight and careful planning: inherently it recoils at opportunism. Throughout the Second World War, however, Axis strategy became riddled by the sort of distorted opportunism that had brought them to power – the waste products of ideology and propaganda.

On June 25 1942, a vast German Army girded itself for a 250 mile drive to the nearest Russian oilfield at Maikop, to those at Baku a further 700 miles beyond, and perhaps to the oil of Iraq yet another 500 miles beyond that, through difficult country. On the same day Panzerarmee, with a mere 60 German tanks and 3,500 infantry, supported by 44 Italian tanks and 6,500 infantry of proven unreliability, stood just 1,100 miles from Iraq and only 550 miles from the pipeline outlets from Iraq at Haifa. Nobody knew how well the Russian Army barring the way to the Caucasus had weathered the winter, but it had not disintegrated: the British Army holding Egypt on the other hand, visibly wilted and, for the moment, possessed few reinforcements close to hand. By opportunist tactics Rommel and Afrika Korps had presented the Axis High Command with the chance to reverse its considered strategy – and tempted it with the gamble of despatching a minute force to the extremity of a maritime and desert supply line, neither of which could be strengthened in the immediate future. But the Axis main effort had been committed alrea to the extremity of its Continent boundary. That was that – it could not brought back just at the stroke of a pen.

Tactically Rommel retained the upp hand – strengthened, indeed, by the arriv of a few of the new Mark IV F tanks wit thicker armour, and a long powerful 75-m gun. The British wavered, for althoug their strong infantry complement wa helped by mounting deliveries of the ne 6-pounder anti-tank gun, this did n offset a depleted tank strength of ju 50 Grants and 100 assorted 2-pounder arme tanks. Experience told them that superiority of 3 to 1 of the latter and parit in Grants was needed to match Afrik Korps – so when Afrika Korps arrived i front of Mersa Matruh on the 25th, th decision to fight nothing sterner than delaying action back to El Alamein ha already been taken – and taken by Auchi leck who, that day, had sent Genera Ritchie on leave and assumed comman of Eighth Army himself.

As a result, when Rommel beat agains Mersa Matruh on the 26th, he timed h intervention to perfection, for he caugh the British Army at the critical momer of a change of command before subordinat commanders had heard or understoo their new superiors' views in detail. More over, the British were also in the process changing their organisation into on whereby brigades took under comman their own artillery (and became Brigad Groups) thus leading to a transitory bu fundamental dilution of that concentratio

Aids to mobility – crossing the Tobruk anti-tank ditch

The counter to mobility – anti-tank mines

87

and flexibility so vital in artillery tactics.

None of this Rommel knew when he launched Afrika Korps on June 26th (the Italians had yet to catch up). He thought the British held a deep minefield with four infantry divisions up to the northern face of the Sidi Hamza escarpment and that 1st Armoured Division shielded the desert flank – whereas, in fact, the British infantry lay thick about Matruh, strong to the south of the escarpment and weak – miserably weak – in the centre, with their armour poised still further south in the desert. Thus Afrika Korps' short outward wheel, intended to brush 1st Armoured Division aside, missed its target but broke through the weak centre instead, while 15th Panzer, on the desert flank, became engaged in a solo battle with the whole

British armoured force supplemented by the New Zealand Division. Had the British been at the top of their form, the whole future of Rommel's advance into Egypt might have been settled there and then: for 15th Panzer should not be expected to defeat a force four times stronger than itself, – and had 15th Panzer disintegrated the fate of 21st Panzer and 90th Light armour in the desert and the British infantry in Matruh, would not have been in doubt.

But General Gott, commanding the British armour in XIIIth Corps, exhibited strange unease as the pressure built up throughout the 27th. Fifteenth Panzer had been checked quite easily, and 21st Panzer as it turned south to take 1st Armoured

Command from the air – a Storch overflies a tank column on the desert road

Division in rear and relieve pressure from 15th Panzer, ran into and was held up by the New Zealand Division where it protected XIIIth Corps' rear. This was hardly surprising since 21st Panzer's tank strength amounted to only 23 tanks and 600 weary infantry, but HQ Eighth Army read the jumble of reports from the desert as those from troops in course of dissolution and decided to launch upon the infantry of Xth Corps at Matruh in a relieving attack. General Gott, meanwhile, also took it that the New Zealanders were breaking up.

Late on the evening of the 27th – at 1900 hours – 90th Light cut the coast road at Ras Hawala, well to the east of Matruh. Half an hour later two British brigades from Matruh were scheduled to attack southwards to assist XIIIth Corps, but at that very moment, General Gott concluded that the time to execute the sort of withdrawal, suggested by Auchinleck's delaying action policy, should begin. At 1920 hours orders to this effect went to 1st Armoured, but not to the New Zealanders – or, astonishingly, for information to HQ Eighth Army.

To Afrika Korps the ensuing events looked something like a miracle. Apart from 90th Light, they had stuck fast – and the delayed arrival of the Italians, Blucher-like, from the west, gave no particular cause for celebration. British infantry attacks debouching from Matruh offered a threat that could be contained with ease by the application of strong artillery fire, but the frowning presence of strong British armour up on the escarpment posed awful possibilities. And then the frown dispersed – and for no apparent reason the British armour rushed eastward leaving Afrika Korps in possession of a battleground they had not conquered, and with the whole of Xth British Corps bottled up in Matruh.

An impartial observer standing on the line of advance of Panzerarmee at the end of June 1942 might have been excused had he rubbed his eyes and wondered who fought who. In the air above there could be no doubt who did what, as wave after wave of RAF bombers flew out from the east, cascaded their bombs on the advancing Axis troops and then returned for more: the Luftwaffe's appearance was but a spasmodic trickle, simply because the Axis advance by land had far outstripped the forward deployment of the Axis airfields. But on land, nearly every unit travelled in British vehicles (and many of the soldiers wore British uniforms regardless of nationality), and the observer would have seen a flood of British trucks, guns, and infantry making for Alamein (and some thought, Palestine) rushing compulsively eastward, stopping here and there merely to snap back at the nearest pursuer. Following these were knots of German armoured cars and motor cyclists preceding a few guns (some of them British 25-pounders), to partake in brief skirmishes with the rearguard, leaving several machines in flames, and more British as prisoners, while a few Germans departed westward in ambulances.

Later came another flurry of British vehicles carrying men who had escaped at the last minute from the trap at Matruh. for Afrika Korps had not had the strength to blockade the town as well as to push on to Alamein, and these soldiers had a hunted, puzzled look – for many had hardly seen the enemy, yet now they fled in perpetual apprehension of ambush from a foe who seemed to infest the coast road. And deep in the sandy expanse to the south crawled the bewildered, ill-controlled remnants of 1st British Armoured Division, out of contact with superior headquarters, and too far off to intervene in the first collision at El Alamein – a fleet in being that lacked purpose.

Then came Afrika Korps itself with a few Italians – the men, vehicles and equipment constituting a dedicated handful that held the future of North Africa, perhaps of the war – and incidentally the reputation of Field-Marshal Rommel – in its grasp. These were men who had crossed the watershed of fatigue – in many cases they were beyond sleep. To their left lapped the sea in which they longed to plunge to wash away the dust which blocked every pore – but there was no time for that. Of their machines, few saw manufacture in Germany or Italy; of their uniform much was made in England a large proportion of their artillery was British, or, in some units, Russian (the captures of the first campaign a year ago). But their tanks were mostly German – some of them veterans of a hundred battles and many dozen repairs, most beginning to run to death at as fast a rate as their crews.

Along the coast road the booty piled up – some, like the petrol, pure gold; whatever it was, however, it became the staple diet of an army starved of native supplies since the beginning, and now grown innured to living off the enemy; this army was, in fact, almost a parasite in the stomach of another. Slowly catching up – it is sad to repeat this of an army which contained many brave men – were the Italians, their officers worried lest again they were headed for destruction.

But the devil himself rode their shoulders – Erwin Rommel, racing backwards and forwards, perched on top of his Mammoth (a captured British vehicle), urging Germans and Italians to the sound of the guns with ruthless determination; thinner than a year ago, not so fit, but wiser, this attack he believed had a chance of success if only the impetus could be maintained.

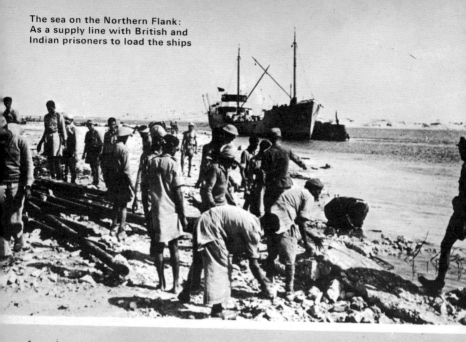

The sea on the Northern Flank:
As a supply line with British and
Indian prisoners to load the ships

As a place to wash away the dust

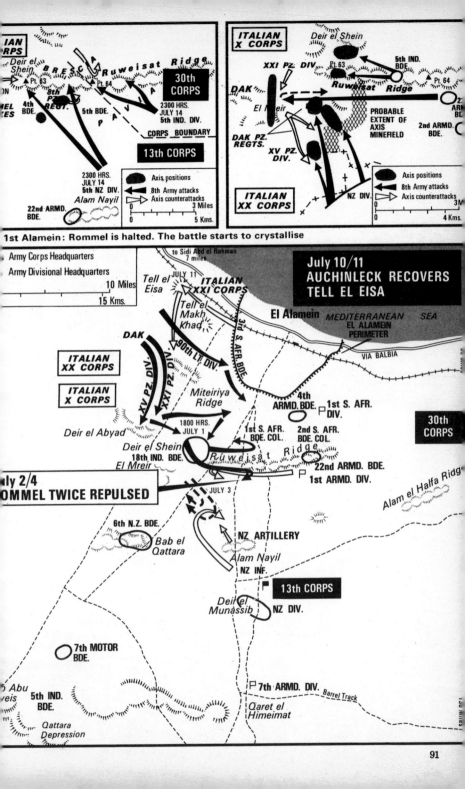

Top left map:

IAN
RPS

B R E S C A

Ruweisat Ridge

Deir el Shein

Pt 63

8th
PZ.
REGT.

Pt 64

30th CORPS

2300 HRS.
JULY 14
5th IND. DIV.

4th BDE.

5th BDE.

P A V I A

CORPS BOUNDARY

13th CORPS

2300 HRS.
JULY 14
5th NZ DIV.

Alam Nayil

22nd ARMD. BDE.

Axis positions
8th Army attacks
Axis counterattacks

3 Miles

5 Kms.

Top right map:

ITALIAN X CORPS

Deir el Shein

5th IND. BDE.

XXI PZ. DIV.

Pt 63

Pt 64

DAK

Ruweisat Ridge

El Mreir

2
ARM
BD

DAK PZ. REGTS.

XV PZ. DIV.

PROBABLE EXTENT OF AXIS MINEFIELD

2nd ARMD. BDE.

ITALIAN XX CORPS

NZ DIV.

Axis positions
8th Army attacks
Axis counterattacks

3

4 Kms.

1st Alamein: Rommel is halted. The battle starts to crystallise

Bottom map:

Army Corps Headquarters

Army Divisional Headquarters

10 Miles

15 Kms.

to Sidi Abd el Rahman
7 miles

JULY 11

Tell el Eisa

ITALIAN XXI CORPS

**July 10/11
AUCHINLECK RECOVERS
TELL EL EISA**

Tell el Makh Khad

3rd S. AFR. BDE.

El Alamein

MEDITERRANEAN   SEA

EL ALAMEIN PERIMETER

DAK

90th LT. DIV.

VIA BALBIA

ITALIAN XX CORPS

ITALIAN X CORPS

XV PZ. DIV.

XXI PZ. DIV.

Miteiriya Ridge

4th ARMD. BDE.

1st S. AFR. DIV.

30th CORPS

1800 HRS. JULY 1

1st S. AFR. BDE. COL.

2nd S. AFR. BDE. COL.

Deir el Abyad

Deir el Shein

Ruweisat Ridge

18th IND. BDE.

El Mreir

22nd ARMD. BDE.

1st ARMD. DIV.

Alam el Halfa Ridge

**ly 2/4
OMMEL TWICE REPULSED**

JULY 3

6th N.Z. BDE.

Bab el Qattara

NZ ARTILLERY

Alam Nayil

NZ INF.

13th CORPS

Deir el Munassib

NZ DIV.

7th MOTOR BDE.

5 Abu
veis

5th IND. BDE.

7th ARMD. DIV.

Barrel Track

Qaret el Himeimat

Qattara Depression

91

The road to Alamein – mixed battle group in every sense including German and British vehicles

The road to Alamein – an 88 mm follows up behind its half-tracked tractor

The actual existence of this weary, glassy-eyed army he felt was not in jeopardy – it could always pull back to safety – but now at least his enemy might crack if once more hustled from the flank and rear as at Matruh. So this was the essence of his policy – avoid direct contact whenever possible, but *lever* the British out of their defences by insinuating Afrika Korps between, around and amongst them. Providing British equipment did not reach parity with his, and if British generalship continued at its current low level – it might be done.

In fact, General Auchinleck's dispositions on the 40 mile gap between the Mediterranean and the salt marsh at Qattara, invited the tactics that Rommel envisaged. Auchinleck just did not have sufficient men to hold a continuous line and could only station his shaken units in commanding positions, hoping that they would stay there long enough to enable his recalcitrant armour to return and intervene effectively against penetrations between the gaps. This was Auchinleck's last chance to assert personal control and discipline upon an army whose command habits resembled a shambling bureaucracy, and whose commanders questioned nearly every order as in committee. Now too he might concentrate and control a strong artillery arm so that it could reach out and tie Afrika Korps in a strait jacket of

shell-fire whenever it moved.

So he strung globules of resistance in diminishing density from the Sea to the Depression asking them to depend for survival on the concentration of gunfire, the co-operation of the armour, their own mobility (since at last they were fully mechanised and not tied to 'boxes'), and the delay that complex minefields might impose upon each German thrust. Given equality in combat worthiness, the on-coming battle must then resolve into a contest of wills between Auchinleck and Rommel – one trying to enmesh the other who must swim free.

90th Light arrived in front of the main Alamein position on the morning of the 30th. Afrika Korps might have been there even quicker had Rommel not directed it through the desert, in the hope of catching fugitives from Matruh, but in the event it brushed inconclusively with 1st Armoured Division – neither side having sufficient vitality to make a serious impression on the other. As was the norm, the Italians lagged behind. General Nehring had his orders to break through by use of the Matruh formula, with 90th Light sent round the Alamein box on the coast while Afrika Korps cut through the desert to isolate and strike the rear of XIIIth Corps – not that Rommel had run out of ideas (although fatigue feeds errors in much the same way as it slows all reactions): he

genuinely believed that only a weak, defeatist enemy opposed him. In any case, supplies were running low and Mussolini, complete with white horse, had arrived in North Africa to lead the Victory Parade through Cairo. The Master must not be kept waiting too long.

Of still greater moment, the German summer offensive had started against the Southern Russian Front on June 28 and although its Causasian objectives had not yet been fully appraised by the British, the first notes of disquiet already disturbed their thinking. If further shaken, the British might be ripe to commit an impulsive, strategic blunder.

Without previous reconnaissance, 90th Light plunged amongst Auchinleck's brigades on the 1st – and, because it knew next to nothing about their layout, ran into rather than around them, becoming embroiled in the very sort of attritional combat they most desired to avoid. Four hours late, partly as a result of bad going, partly the product of fatigue, Afrika Korps blundered into yet another defended locality south of 90th Light (the Deir el Shein position) and, instead of diverging, took the line of greatest resistance by trying to storm it. To their dismay, it held them up for the rest of the day, and though British armour failed to turn up, the depth of the whole Alamein position now began to reveal itself, when each

eastward bound brought down a hail of shell fire from an enemy who no longer stood foot-fast as of old. And when later that day the British armour, which had stayed placid up to then, crept cautiously along Ruweisat Ridge towards Deir el Shein, it drove 15th Panzer before it.

By July 2, any hope Rommel may have had of bursting past El Alamein, as at Matruh, had vanished. Another deliberate, carefully prepared, assault as at Gazala would be needed, but as once had been the case at Tobruk in April 1941, neither the resources nor the time were available. South of Ruweisat Ridge, XIIIth British Corps began to exert pressure at the very moment when Afrika Korps started to shift east again, in parallel with 21st Panzer to the north of the Ridge. Neither got very far, even though they prompted the symptomatic chorus of unhappy woe amongst the tired British commanders. But though Rommel knew he had shot his bolt, he still called on Afrika Korps for yet another last heave northwards on July 3, sending XXth Italian Corps ('Ariete' and 'Trieste') in a flank attack to the south designed to hold off XIIIth Corps. He might have saved himself this misguided effort, for the Afrika Korps could hardly achieve on the 3rd what it had failed to do on the 1st over the same ground in greater strength; and the Italians simply ran headlong into an artillery barrage that stopped them dead, exposing them to an annihilating counter-attack by New Zealand infantry with the bayonet.

As an offensive instrument Afrika Korps, and thereby Panzerarmee, now lost its credibility. Left for a while to regather its strength behind the Italian infantry divisions (who were moving up to establish a solid front from the sea as far inland as possible), it might later recover the initiative for Rommel, but at this moment it was hard pressed to bolster the Italians whose numbers had shrunk disastrously since Gazala. In fact, one good British counter-attack, then and there, might have over-turned the entire Axis structure, for most 'German' artillery ammunition was British; German-built guns only had two rounds each, and the total tank strength of Afrika Korps totalled only 50. Indeed, on July 4, 15th Panzer was practically chased off Ruweisat Ridge by 1st Armoured – the latter then coming to an ignominious halt at the crack of a few 88s from a lay-back position.

Neither side for the moment possessed the will to continue – let alone the strength – but there was one significant difference between them: whereas Afrika Korps could only scrape up reinforcements and go on employing its old, tired personnel and equipment, Eighth Army would soon enjoy an infusion of fresh men and material and be able to withdraw its exhausted elements.

Australians began to take over Ruweisat Ridge: 7th Armoured Division, equipped to a lighter scale, took over the southern flank; unblooded formations disembarked from ships in the Canal Zone; and the Royal Air Force stepped up its attacks across the entire battle area, repeatedly cutting the Axis coastal supply route even by night. Satisfied that Rommel had met a crisis, and confident that his own troops might now advance, Auchinleck began a series of attacks on July 10. Unfortunately for Rommel they occurred at the very moment and place where he least expected them, for he had conditioned himself to believe that all British action would be hesitant, retrograde and lacking in subtlety. So when the New Zealanders withdrew on the southern flank from Bab el Qattara for tactical convenience, Rommel followed up hard next day with 21st Panzer behind a furious bombardment aimed at the evacuated positions, with visions of yet another dramatic wheel against a crumbling enemy rear conjured up before him.

This was opportunism gone mad: Afrika Korps could not yet sustain offensive operations – if only for mechanical reasons, since its tanks were running at their last gasp. Unnoticed, the initiative had slipped away from Rommel, and a heavy attack on the night of July 10 by the Australians broke the Italian 'Sabratha' Division and left none in doubt that this was the case;

General Cruewell
General von Bismark

only by the intervention of the newly arrived German 164th Division from Crete, led in person by von Mellenthin of Panzerarmee's staff, was a complete rout averted. Caught miles from the critical point, Rommel turned about and rushed off northward, picking up part of 15th Panzer on the way, and flinging it against the unyielding flank of the Australian attack; but now Afrika Korps danced to the British tune.

In fact, Auchinleck's attack had been carefully selected to fall upon Italians. 'Sabratha' fell in ruins, and then 'Trieste' took a severe blow, sucking the tired Germans to their rescue out of reserve into the battle line again. Once more attack and counter-attack swayed to and fro in the vicinity of El Alamein, and again stalemate settled in a strait-jacket of raging artillery fire, amidst the cloying minefields. But even though Rommel might strive to keep Afrika Korps in reserve, he could no longer leave Italians 'uncorseted' by German troops. The old 'stays' system, initiated at Gazala, returned.

Wherever Italians stood, there the British attacks might be expected, (the next one of any consequence falling upon 'Brescia' and 'Pavia' on Ruweisat Ridge) and thus within a year British policy had turned a somersault. At the beginning of 'Crusader', Afrika Korps had acted as the opposite end of a magnet attracting British armour: now the presence of Afrika Korps repelled British armour as if of similar polarity. Quite often, of course, Afrika Korps did manage to catch up with a British attack, but by then the British had usually established a defensive position strong enough to foil, at low cost, whatever counter the Germans devised. Realising this, Rommel did more than integrate picked men with the Italians – he began to station complete Afrika Korps formations tightly within the Italian sectors, thus reducing the distance they must travel to intercept British incursions; simultaneously, he aimed to slow down every aggression by sowing high density minefields between the Qattara Depression and the sea and although fighting continued to centre on the ridges because these gave the best observation, a man-made tactical feature thus appeared.

Indian troops attacked 'Pavia' on the Ruweisat Ridge on the night of the 14th while the 2nd New Zealand Division took on 'Brescia', debouching from the open desert in the south. At first, HQ Panzerarmee, its attention rivetted on an action being fought by 21st Panzer to reduce the Australian penetration near the coast, assessed the attack at Ruweisat as no more than a raid. But with the dawn the awful completeness of the disaster that had struck both Italian divisions became evident. Stragglers pressed back, spreading panic to the rear, and the whole ridge seemed to

Other people's tanks. British Valentines destroyed on Ruweisat Ridge

Other people's soldiers. The British surrendering near Alamein

40

have fallen into British hands, for the New Zealanders' attack had passed right through 8th Panzer Regiment where it lingered in the dark to the south of the ridge.

Reacting with verve, however, its commander set about a New Zealand battalion, wiped out its anti-tank guns and departed with his prisoners to join Afrika Korps' concentration on the western lee of the ridge, thus reversing the flow of battle. Had the British been able to launch their armour on the heels of the infantry success a rout could have ensued – but mines, uncertainty, a bit of malaise and a lot of under-confidence kept the British armour back, with the result that nothing withstood a positive hurricane of German artillery fire which now swept the ridge as a precursor to a characteristic Afrika Korps charge that retook the lost ground with 1,200 New Zealanders as prisoners. Twenty thousand Italians had waited, ready packed, to be escorted to Cairo: now they ran free watching their late captors being dragged off instead. Materially honours were about even: psychologically the British armour lost its honour, their feeble performance, prompting a New Zealand Brigadier to voice Eighth Army's 'most intense distrust, almost hatred' of it.

Of course, the British tank crews were old, wily desert birds who imbibed a natural caution from bitter experience; it takes green troops to make the rashest advances. By July 21, Auchinleck had a supply – 23rd Armoured Brigade, quite fresh from the United Kingdom, mounted in new, critically under-gunned Valentine tanks. The venue selected for their first performance was Ruweisat Ridge – the method, an attack from east to west with Indian infantry, after the New Zealanders had cleared the enemy up its southern slopes. What slight resemblance there existed between this and the plan of the previous assault possessed only marginal significance, for the entire sector had since been occupied by Afrika Korps, the mines lay thicker, the ring of anti-tank guns tighter and better concealed, and the whole Axis armour clung close to the front, poised for immediate counter-attack. Lacking in faith, the New Zealanders hardly bothered to make arrangements with the armour (which so frequently failed to keep its appointments) and failed themselves to open adequate gaps in the minefields to let the armour through to their aid.

Few desert attacks thus had less chance of success than this one. Nehring, on the morning of July 22 after overrunning the armour-bare New Zealanders and watching 23rd Armoured Brigade press in tight formation along the southern edge of Ruweisat, strewing tanks on mines and dying in scores before the raging 88s, might have repeated Wellington's words – 'They came on in the same old way and we stopped them in the same old way'. Everywhere including their participation in an Australian raid against Miteiriya Ridge, 23rd Armoured Brigade left a trail of wrecked machinery, losing well over 100 tanks and over 200 men in actions characterised by supreme gallantry and utter stupidity. Rommel's fading hopes rose accordingly, recognising this considerable defensive success as a stabilising factor to his slowly coalescing defence.

More British attacks were to come – none as costly as that of the 22nd: air raids abounded and raids by long range desert parties repeatedly disturbed tenuous lines of communication, but Rommel's immediate crisis had passed and he could concentrate on long-term planning instead of improvisation. But here the position was still not encouraging. Marshals Kesselring and Cavallero had called to see Rommel just when Afrika Korps' resources had fallen to their lowest level; no longer then was it a case of calling for specific items since everything from men to tanks and clothing to petrol came from the dregs. Perversely, the only substantial reinforcement that might be found consisted of those very airborne forces earmarked for 'Hercules' against Malta in September and Kesselring clung grimly to that operation, pointing out that more men in Africa merely placed a still greater load on supply lines that faltered before aggression from the island.

Kesselring's awful dilemma is best expressed in his own words. 'Even I was eventually forced to decide against it [Hercules] as the premises for success were just no longer there. The calling off of this undertaking was a mortal blow to the whole North Africa undertaking. I now urged the resumption of the offensive as vigorously as I had intervened after Tobruk to break it off.'

Afrika Korps' triumph and fate clasped it to El Alamein. Fresh blood – not a torrent, but flowing thick enough to restore colour – began to trickle in, and with it a new arrogance at HQ Panzerarmee which had never been there in the pioneering days. Prestige now became coupled with real achievement, making the slightest withdrawal or loss of face hard to allow – a point of view urged and condoned by Hitler in Berlin. Meanwhile, Mussolini betook himself back to Rome, the triumphant entry into Cairo in abeyance.

Battle of frustration

The turbulent deadlock at Ruweisat brought Mr Churchill and his advisers to understand that the existence of Panzerarmee so close to Egypt threatened British prestige in the Middle East to an extent hardly before envisaged. The balance of Middle Eastern strategy rocked. If the Suez Base changed hands, terrible repercussions must follow over and above the wasting effects of the cessation of British seaborne traffic through the Mediterranean. For if the German drive out of Russia, pressing – so it seemed – almost unopposed towards the Caucasus, met Afrika Korps in Iraq and linked with the Japanese raiding the Indian Ocean and Peninsular, a total collapse of Allied resistance might well ensue. En route for Moscow for a bitter meeting with Stalin, Churchill stopped off at Cairo on August 3 to examine matters first hand. As he saw it, Rommel merely awaited the first convenient opportunity to continue his advance. Because Auchinleck had failed, he had lost Churchill's confidence. Within a few days General Alexander had taken his place as Commander-in-Chief, while General Montgomery took command of Eighth Army.

These events, momentous for the British, only percolated slowly to Rommel's attention and probably titillated Afrika Korps' vanity as just one more moral victory to them, for of the desert commanders only Rommel survived. The Afrika Korps could claim, moreover, that their lost commanders had been killed, wounded, or taken prisoner; not sacked. HQ Panzerarmee certainly seems to have been slow in appraising its new opponents; but, after all, Alexander had only won distinction by executing tidy withdrawals in harrowing circumstances, and Montgomery had next to no reputation outside the British Army, though Rommel might have been more intrigued had he known that Montgomery, a fellow infantryman, had, like him, written official infantry instructional manuals. Thus Rommel, an intuitive expert in mobile warfare, found himself against an expert in positional warfare whose knowledge of armoured techniques stemmed from study and tactical exercises.

With the German High Command belatedly demanding that Rommel should stay at Alamein where his presence posed a complementary threat to the German advance to the Caucasus, Rommel's attention focused primarily on acquiring the huge increases in supplies and reinforcements of all kinds that had been promised him. But as usual, difficulties arose in fulfilling those promises. Malta still survived – though under heavy pressure from the Luftwaffe and its power to interrupt the supply routes had certainly declined. However, Malta was still important, for Panzerarmee's supplies still came through Tripoli and Benghazi, and now they had to be transported an additional 600 miles to the front. The nearest port – Tobruk – could only reduce that distance by 300 miles, and in any case could barely handle 600 tons a day – a tithe of the full requirements. Moreover, the coastal road lay wide open to interdiction by aircraft and raiding parties: it frequently erupted with burning

The promised land – an Afrika Korps
crew looks towards Cairo

Other people's transport. A German platoon carried in a British truck

But the infantry find it hard going

The Royal Air Force takes over. Afrika Korps moves towards the Alam Halfa Ridge, but the RAF carpets them with bombs and the vital petrol burns

lorries. Reinforcement by air from Crete had advantages (164th German Division, the Ramcke Parachute Brigade and the Italian Folgore Airborne Division all came that way after 'Hercules' had been cancelled) but as a reliable source of bulk supply it failed.

Rommel's writings at this time are those of a despondent man – albeit a very sick one too. He expanded a catalogue of woe, castigating Italian and German administrators as far back as Tripoli and across the whole expanse of Europe, for failing to meet his demands, commenting bitterly on the manner in which Italian units seemed to receive their supplies, while the long suffering Afrika Korps went without. In one breath he described manpower shortages amongst the Italian infantry and the next reviled them for sending a complete new infantry formation to the theatre.

Yet in fact his strength did increase, both in quantity and quality; by August 30 Afrika Korps possessed 166 Mark III tanks (73 of them with the long 50-mm gun) and 37 Mark IVs (27 of them Specials with the long 75-mm gun). His outpourings are thus those of a desperate man whose physical condition had reduced him to despair, they are also sincere – those of a general who hated to impose frustration on soldiers who had served him so well.

Now, once more, Rommel had to throw them into battle under less propitious conditions than ever before – although not entirely without hope. Allowing for the fact that most British supplies travelled the long route round the Cape of Good Hope, HQ Panzerarmee calculated that the losses incurred by the enemy in June would not be replaced until mid-September. If Afrika Korps could launch a supreme effort at the beginning of the month, it might thus achieve the sort of spoiling victory at which it specialised, for they knew of nothing that had altered the relative merits of their own battle craft compared with that of the British. The twin keys to victory, so far as the Germans imagined them, remained armour and supplies. Providing their technically superior armour could be established in the enemy rear long enough to break the British will to resist, the Alamein position might collapse, mobile warfare might resume, unbarring the way to copious supplies in the Delta.

Intelligence sources indicated that a

wide gap covered only by mines and light forces existed on the southern flank of the British position, between the Qattara Depression and Alam Nayil: if that gap could be rapidly breached, Afrika Korps might drive east and then north to cut the coast road at El Hamman, having passed east of the Alam Halfa Ridge, then known to be held by Eighth Army.

Rommel hoped to achieve victory by surprise, beginning with a penetration through 30 miles of unreconnoitred mine-strewn ground at night. He lacked reserves in manpower and machines – above all he lacked petrol reserves even though, only four days before the attack, Cavallero had told Rommel, 'You can begin the battle now, the petrol is already under way.' But the 6,000 tons he referred to never arrived in time – most of it sank in a torpedoed tanker off Tobruk.

A dreadful inevitability telegraphed every Axis move to the British. Even without the Royal Air Force detecting the first signs of a build-up on the southern sector, they could calculate the outline of Rommel's tactics. They realised that, since he did not possess a reliable infantry mass Rommel was unlikely to engage in a head-

on assault against the strong British infantry positions in the north: short of time and strong in armour, he must seek room for manoeuvre and therefore could only approach via the south. Montgomery then had only to guess at the depth and strength of his outflanking swing. Nevertheless, by stationing strong forces on the Alam Halfa Ridge, with his armoured reserve in its shelter, Montgomery, at best, hoped to persuade Rommel into making a direct assault on this prepared position, or, at worst, to thrust the German armoured forces into the open where they could be engaged when at the extremities of their over-stretched supply lines. Either way it would be attrition – but always in Montgomery's favour for he had no intention of being drawn into the sort of fast moving free-for-all at which Rommel and Afrika Korps excelled: keeping clear of a dog fight also gave his air forces more space in which to pick their targets.

Afrika Korps' concentration opposite the 'gap' lost its secret before last light on the 30th. Thereafter, as it struggled eastward by moonlight through the minefields and the screening British forces, lit by flares and bombarded in the rear by the RAF, it

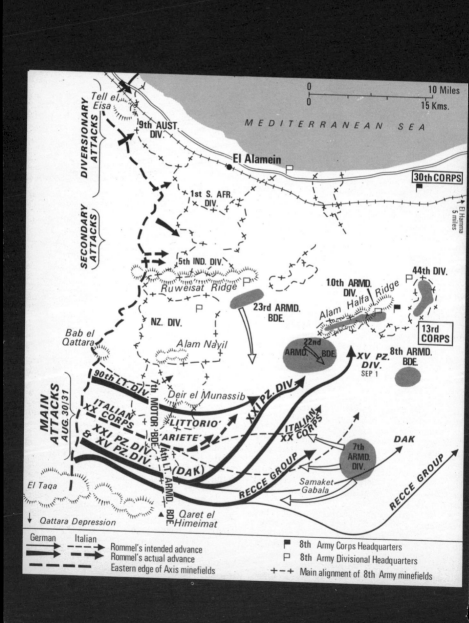

MEDITERRANEAN SEA

DIVERSIONARY ATTACKS

SECONDARY ATTACKS

MAIN ATTACKS AUG. 30/31

0 ——— 10 Miles
0 ——— 15 Kms.

Tell el Eisa

9th AUST. DIV.

El Alamein

30th CORPS

El Hamma 5 miles

1st S. AFR. DIV.

5th IND. DIV.

Ruweisat Ridge

23rd ARMD. BDE.

NZ. DIV.

Alam Nayil

10th ARMD. DIV.

44th DIV.

Alam Halfa Ridge

13rd CORPS

Bab el Qattara

22nd ARMD. BDE.

XV PZ. DIV. SEP 1

8th ARMD. BDE.

90th LT. DIV.

7th MOTOR BDE.

Deir el Munassib

XXI PZ. DIV.

ITALIAN XX CORPS

'LITTORIO'

'ARIETE'

ITALIAN XX CORPS

DAK

XXI PZ. DIV. & XV PZ. DIV.

4th LT. ARMD. BDE.

(DAK)

7th ARMD. DIV.

RECCE GROUP

Samaket Gabala

El Taqa

▲ Qaret el Himeimat

RECCE GROUP

↓ Qattara Depression

German   Italian
➡ ➡➡➡   Rommel's intended advance
➡ ➡ ➡   Rommel's actual advance
– – –   Eastern edge of Axis minefields
+ – +   Main alignment of 8th Army minefields

🚩 8th Army Corps Headquarters
⌐ 8th Army Divisional Headquarters

endured a non-stop harassing fire. The tight schedule fell into arrears as uncharted minefields and seas of loose sand clogged progress, causing concertinering, confusion and exhaustion, besides an unforeseen over-consumption of petrol. Critical periods such as these demand the imposition of forceful leadership – and in the past Rommel would have been there in the thick of it; but this time he held back, a sick man, listening to the reports as they trickled in. Up at the front General Nehring lay wounded at HQ Afrika Korps and General von Bismarck, commanding 21st Panzer, had been killed by a mine. Although Colonel Bayerlein, Afrika Korps Chief of Staff, took immediate charge and forged slowly ahead, the leading troops had barely cleared the minefields by dawn, leaving a trail of mined vehicles in their train.

There really was not much point in going on. All surprise had been lost, Afrika Korps squatted in the south with XXth Italian Corps and 90th Light Division on its northern flank bunched in confusion; petrol ran low and the whole group, caught in solitary state well clear of the enemy, lay wide open to unrestricted aerial bombardment. The wide sweep to El Hamman could no longer be attempted – the choice was now simply between prudence and recklessness, sane withdrawal or a gambler's advance.

As he set out for the front Rommel had remarked to his doctor, 'The decision to attack to-day is the hardest I have ever taken. Either the army in Russia succeeds in getting through to Grozny and we in Africa manage to reach the Suez Canal or . . . ' and he made a gesture of defeat. So his decision to persevere in the face of defeat on the morning of August 31 is not difficult to understand: it was one of desperation – a last fling made doubly uncertain because

it could only be directed against the strongest sector on the Alam Halfa Ridge. In one respect, Afrika Korps old luck held when a sandstorm blew up which blotted out their movements from the attention of the hostile bombers. Then under the command of General von Vaerst (in Nehring's absence), it gathered itself and shuffled piecemeal in the general direction of its objective, but deprived of information since the Reconnaissance Groups were fully employed holding off the 7th Armoured Division, flitting menacingly about the exposed eastern flank. So instead of hitting a well reconnoitred position with all its resources concentrated, Panzerarmee merely sent Afrika Korps on a death-ride against the strongest portion of undisclosed enemy defences.

Fifteenth Panzer led the way, ignoring a covey of Crusader tanks which took flight under their noses and headed off to the north, but concentrating instead on outflanking the British position to the east. Twenty-first Panzer followed and, in due course, 'Littorio' and 'Ariete' began to arrive on their left. But across the horizon a moving barrier of British armour began to reveal itself and, from concealed gun pits, anti-tank guns swung their muzzles and let drive in unison against the fumbling Afrika Korps. In attempting to close with the dug-in tanks on the ridge, Afrika Korps exposed itself to the full fury of the 6-pounder guns, thus falling into a trap at the vital point, beset by an enemy superior in numbers, position and technique.

Tanks burned on both sides, some of the anti-tank guns were overrun, but, in effect, the Alam Halfa Ridge, its defences never accurately appreciated by the Germans, was barely encroached upon, and as night approached, von Vaerst broke off the token attack. So far as Afrika Korps was con-

The lost battlefield:
British infantry advances past a burning Pz Kw III

cerned no alternative remained – their losses had not been crushing but the acute shortage of petrol more or less stalled them and made it uncertain that they could even retire. An extraordinary calm descended momentarily on the forward edge of the battle. Rommel spent the night deciding what to do next: Montgomery adjusted his position and stolidly refused to be drawn into a frenzied counter charge.

But in the Axis rear, as the dust storm subsided, the RAF started work again, subjecting the Axis to a pummelling such as they had never experienced before. Hour after hour it went on with the mounting toll of wrecked equipment second in importance only to the shock inflicted on the minds of men whose composure was rattled from concussion and loss of sleep.

Rommel should have withdrawn on the night of the 31st but his powers of rapid decision seem to have deserted him. He clung to hope, not reason, hoping Montgomery might commit military suicide in the manner of his predecessors, wishing above all that sufficient petrol might arrive to save his army. Nothing of the sort transpired, so early on September 1 he cancelled all large-scale movements, settling instead for a few local attacks in the Micawberish hope of something turning up, merely exposing his men to another 24 hours of pitiless bombing. Driving through the forward zone that morning amongst burning and wrecked vehicles, Rommel underwent the same constant aerial attack himself and returned to his HQ a shaken man.

Just enough petrol to return safely to his own lines remained; the diversionary attacks against the British infantry on the coast had failed, so it could only be a few hours before the full force of a counter blow struck Afrika Korps. He could wait no longer.

Already ominous movements stirred to the west of El Alamein, where Australian infantry projected raids typical of those which had studded Auchinleck's July offensive. Should the front be broken here, with Afrika Korps miles away and even behind the enemy lines, the whole of Panzerarmee might fall into jeopardy for lack of a mobile reserve. Nevertheless, Rommel's plan of withdrawal exhibited a cool, defiant caution, moving systematically from bound to bound in his determination not to be rushed in order to avoid the sort of disorder which leads to panic.

In so much as Montgomery tried at all to cut off Rommel's retreat, the blocking of the exits through the minefields alone took form. Even then the operation was not timed to take place until the night of September 3, and by then Afrika Korps' withdrawal was well under way, with its northern flank heavily guarded and the Luftwaffe playing a more strenuous part in breaking up the constant series of bombing raids. Everything now slowly centred on that critical piece of desert between Deir el Munassib and Quarat el Himeimat, the clouds of dust and smoke rising thickly from the constant bombardment and the intense movement taking place there.

Attacks launched by British and New Zealand infantry with Valentine tanks at

10.30pm on the 3rd became channelled within the confines of thick minefields and along narrow corridors – exactly where the German and Italians expected them. A British infantry brigade straggled late and unprepared into this, its first action – lending point to Montgomery's contention that many of his troops were unready for an offensive – and a curtain of defensive fire closed across the front. The British faltered, although where the New Zealander pierced the defences heavy fighting broke out, but barely a flutter arose at HQ Panzerarmee, although reports of 1,000 casualties inflicted on their attackers left no doubt that this had been a serious attempt which might be repeated.

Nevertheless, the battle ended to Rommel's timetable when, on September 6, he went over to the defensive amongst the positions seized from the British at the outset. Fighting guttered out, the tanks and guns holding each other off at long range, the artillery fire slackening and dying away, while air sorties became smaller and less violent amongst sandstorms, with fewer targets to attack in the face of mounting fighter opposition. Casualties had come out about even – Rommel's heavier tank losses up by Alam Halfa ridge compensated later by the heavy loss of Valentine tanks near Deir el Munassib. At the last, Afrika Korps seemed to emerge in command of the situation, with its reputation unscathed since the official German announcements called the operation only a reconnaissance in force.

But Pride had taken a tumble, in no way assuaged by Rommel's excuses to his wife that the action had to be broken off for supply reasons and the superiority of the enemy air force ' – although victory was otherwise ours.'

Rommel's soldiers called it 'The Six Day Race'. Montgomery viewed it as an inevitable interlude in his preparations for his own battle of annihilation – and considers it a model in the defensive mode. Whatever praise is to be lavished on the British commander and his troops for their steadiness at a vital moment – perhaps the turning point in the desert war – must be qualified by equal praise of Afrika Korps tempered with sharp criticism of Rommel's direction of the battle. From the beginning it never looked a practical operation of war, lacking sufficient power, surprise or sustenance. Thoroughly direct in its application, it imposed no serious problems or strain upon the defence.

Of course, by the end of August, the entire Axis position in Africa was a false one. Having failed to give sufficient support to enable Egypt to be taken in one bound, the correct course would have been a withdrawal to the natural strong defences at Halfaya. Since that did not satisfy the shifting Axis politico/military policy, the attack on the Alam Halfa ridge should have been stopped once its element of surprise evaporated during the first night. To remain, almost passive, for a further 48 hours exposed to all sorts of fire after the initial repulse, depicted a quite uncharacteristic malaise on Rommel's part – the signature of a sick man.

Field-Marshal Erwin Rommel receives his baton from a grateful Fuehrer.

Second Alamein: without the initiative

Rommel knew, and so did Montgomery, that the Battle of Alam Halfa marked the irrevocable transfer of the initiative from Panzerarmee to Eighth Army. Of course, a few weeks elapsed before the fact became common knowledge, but the subsequent dispositions adopted by the Axis left Afrika Korps in no doubt that, from then on, theirs was to be a waiting, defensive role, while the intensive preparations going on behind the British lines were wholly offensive.

Vast mountains of material and shiploads of men accumulated at Montgomery's command. Relays of bombers and fighters took off with rising tempo to blast the Axis sea and land supply lines, their airfields and their gun positions. At the front the defended localities acted only as a shield for the aggressive regrouping going on behind – and the men who were to take part, from commander to trooper, realised that the coming assault – timed for full moon on October 23 – would be crushing.

Montgomery planned in great simplicity – aiming to fix Afrika Korps' attention with diversionary attacks against the seemingly, more vulnerable southern flank, while swamping the more heavily defended localities between Tell el Eisa and Miteiriya Ridge with artillery fire of unprecedented fury, as the prelude to assault by infantry. Then engineers would clear corridors through the minefields along which an armoured corps of two armoured divisions could pass to occupy the commanding Kidney and Miteiriya Ridges. Against these ridges Montgomery hoped to tempt Afrika Korps into a series of attacks, emulating the sort of self destruction that had taken place at Alam Halfa. It is interesting that Montgomery seems to have read Rommel's mind with an insight that told him that Rommel would fight it out and not withdraw. For as yet neither Hitler's no-withdrawal phobia, nor a radical change in Axis desert strategy advertised itself.

Rommel returned to Austria, via Berlin, for medical treatment on September 23, handing over temporary command of Panzerarmee to General von Thoma, one of the original Panzer pioneers, until General Stumme could transfer from the Russian front: whereupon von Thoma was to take command of Afrika Korps. Before he left, Rommel spent a busy fortnight organising the front for defence, indoctrinating Stumme and von Thoma in the mysteries of a war such as neither had experienced before, and badgering superior officers from Kesselring to Cavallero, and Mussolini to Hitler, for the supplies without which hopes of survival, let alone victory, must collapse.

Overture to El Alamein. RAF Baltimores soften up the Afrika Korps

In the fat, red-faced Stumme Rommel felt no confidence – the man's experience stemmed from Russia and he discounted the special conditions associated with fighting in the desert, against the well-equipped British. The plan of defence was Rommel's – an extension of the policy of 'corseting' Italian with German formations, creating two layers of battlegroups along the length and breadth of the front. Now, for the first time, Afrika Korps became split so as to merge with Italian Armoured Divisions – 15th Panzer with 'Littorio' in the north and 21st Panzer with 'Ariete' in the south – with each of these groups split into three.

Minefield barriers caged entrenched infantry amidst walls of defensive artillery-fire. The armour, kept close in rear, was to act as a helper by countering penetrations as they occurred – a reversal of all Rommel's previous techniques: clearly the shortage of petrol had something to do with this, but the wholesale destruction which might be meted out by a hostile air force against mobile troops in the open desert seemed overriding. Only so long as the armour remained concealed, or in close combat, might it escape attention by aircraft in daylight: all large-scale movements would have to make use of the cover of darkness and hope to avoid detection by enemy flares.

Rommel and Afrika Korps thus became the first German contingent to come to grips with the sort of Allied air supremacy that was soon to overlay every battlefield. Quicker than most to detect and counter new trends, Rommel was to find immense difficulty in convincing his colleagues in Europe of the true implications of the Anglo-American material superiority. In the meantime, the Axis soldiery, beset by acute self-preservative inclinations, learned to dig deeper and keep an eye constantly cocked skywards for hostile aircraft – the 'German Glance' as they called it'– for the Luftwaffe flew less than ever before.

Unhappily, the health of Afrika Korps suffered too, partly as the result of an unimaginative diet, and many of the most experienced leaders went home for rest and recuperation. However, morale stayed remarkably high, although it would be interesting to know how Afrika Korps' soldiers might have felt had they known that their combined strength of 104,000 (including 54,000 Italians), 489 tanks (including only 30 Mark IV Specials and 278 obsolete Italian machines) and 675 aircraft (only 275 Germans) was pitted against 195,000 British with over a thousand tanks and 750 aircraft. Moreover the arrival of the new American built Sherman tank now introduced an element of technical surprise hardly less potent than the superior techniques applied by the British to an

The building of an artificial
barrier. A German laying mines

The British barrage opens on October 23, while their infantry wait to assault

artillery complement twice the size of Panzerarmee's.

The day before Montgomery struck at El Alamein, General Stumme had been presenting medals to the Italians and exhorting them to do their duty. Overhead the bombers passed in ceaseless procession to hammer the airfields and supply dumps in the rear. Grimly aware that the supreme moment could not be delayed much longer, and only too conscious that the supply situation had worsened and that he was sustained mainly by the residue of stores captured in June, Stumme awaited the worst that might befall.

At 2130 hours on October 23 a storm of artillery fire engulfed the Axis front, concentrated heaviest in the north where the main British effort centred, but in considerable volume elsewhere. As in the nature of night actions, the situation only slowly resolved itself at the operational headquarters. Control centralised somewhat clumsily upon Stumme at HQ Panzerarmee, while HQ of Afrika Korps shared a locality with HQ XXth Corps mid-way between their two widely separated armoured groups, playing only a watching role at this stage and epitomising the impotence to which fuel shortages had reduced them. Short of information, Stumme went at dawn – not to HQ Afrika Korps – but to HQ 90th Light Division near the coast, came under shell-fire, collapsed and died of a heart attack. It cannot be said that his presence was greatly missed.

By afternoon of the 24th, a pattern of battle could be assembled. A British sub-

Exhorted to resist. Italian officers decorated by the Germans

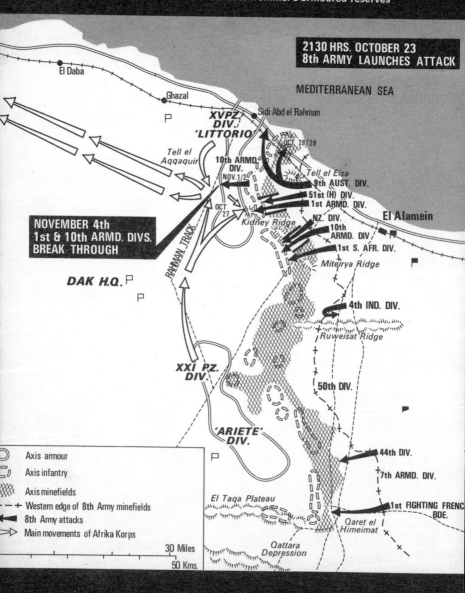

2nd Alamein: 8th Army wears down and defeats Rommel's armoured reserves

2130 HRS. OCTOBER 23 8th ARMY LAUNCHES ATTACK

MEDITERRANEAN SEA

El Daba

Ghazal

Sidi Abd el Rahman

P

XVPZ DIV. 'LITTORIO'

OCT. 28/29

Tell el Aqqaquir

10th ARMD. DIV.

NOV.1/2

Tell el Eisa

9th AUST. DIV.

51st (H) DIV.

1st ARMD. DIV.

OCT 27

NZ. DIV.

El Alamein

Kidney Ridge

10th ARMD. DIV.

1st S. AFR. DIV.

NOVEMBER 4th 1st & 10th ARMD. DIVS. BREAK THROUGH

Miteirya Ridge

DAK H.Q. P

P

4th IND. DIV.

Ruweisat Ridge

XXI PZ. DIV.

50th DIV.

'ARIETE' DIV.

P

44th DIV.

7th ARMD. DIV.

El Taqa Plateau

1st FIGHTING FRENC BDE.

Qaret el Himeimat

Qattara Depression

Axis armour

Axis infantry

Axis minefields

Western edge of 8th Army minefields

8th Army attacks

Main movements of Afrika Korps

30 Miles

50 Kms.

sidiary attack in the south had virtually come to a halt amongst the minefields, permitting 21st Panzer and 'Ariete' to remain optimistically uncommitted, but in the northern gap, 15th Panzer/'Littorio's southern group became uneasily aware that the enemy had installed infantry and armour on Miteiriya Ridge, and thus threatened the stability of their entire locality – and perhaps of the front as a whole. Still more threatening seemed a hole being drilled by Highlanders and Australians towards Kidney Ridge (an almost undefinable feature but vital to 15th Panzer's centre group because it lay in the heart of its territory). The bombardment by British guns and aircraft went on without pause while, in the midst, the Axis armoured battlegroups, supported by a rising volume of artillery and anti-tank fire of their own, reacted strongly against each principal incursion.

In Germany a call from Hitler propelled Rommel out of his sanatorium, physical cure incomplete, but his whole heart and mind leaping out to Africa. Next evening found him back at the front, in his wake a number of shattered Italian and German administrators who had been left in no doubt that, unless more supplies could be sent, Panzerarmee must be doomed. In the meantime von Thoma had held command, fighting on the restrictive lines laid down by Rommel and perpetuated by Stumme – and not without success, for each British penetration beyond the line reached on the first day had been hurled back, marking the approaches to Miteiriya and Kidney Ridge with the stain from dozens of burning tanks. Losses amongst the German armour, though heavy enough, had not yet become crippling, but the ability of the new Sherman tanks to stand out of harm's way and shell the exposed and vulnerable 88s, was a worrying factor which had already proved fatal.

A British appreciation had already concluded that the enemy would not readily withdraw: Rommel went further and stated that the British must be thrown out with a view to re-occupying the original positions – a fundamental decision because it pitched Afrika Korps out of prepared positions into the open, in a series of ripostes of the very sort that Montgomery most desired in order to shoot up the German armour. Already Rommel exhibited the old depression, noticeable during Alam Halfa, by demostrating that, in a tight, positional battle, he performed below his best. Von Thoma observed the repeated changes of mind – a habit reflected in Rommel's own account for October 26 when, on one line, he declares that to remove forces from the south would be unthinkable because of the fuel shortage, the next records his decision to bring 21st Panzer north, and at the end of the paragraph touches on the gradual

redeployment from south to north of more and more artillery.

To Montgomery the arrival of 21st Panzer close to Kidney Ridge on the 27th acted as a tonic, but the eruption of this beautifully trained formation amongst his army might have been highly disquieting, had not numbers been so disproportionately in the British favour, and a single British battalion stood its ground and destroyed upward of 30 tanks. This attack by 21st Panzer represented Rommel's main attempt to throw the British back into the minefields, but all it did was impose further delay at the price of irreplaceable tank losses. Along with the infantry, Afrika Korps began to crumble away – its strength on the 28th a mere 81 tanks, its role in battle lacking concentration.

It had always been Montgomery's intention to lure Afrika Korps to an act of self-destruction, thereby depriving the Axis infantry of mobile protection and exposing them to a simple mopping-up operation. But by the 27th it had become apparent, despite Montgomery's confident assertions, that the Afrika Korps was not yet spent, that British armour had not won its freedom of action, and that four days' pummelling had undermined his own infantry's enthusiasm.

In these circumstances, Montgomery varied his policy by throwing more weight into night assaults aimed at the German defences near the coast. Fifteenth Panzer with 90th Light were already deeply involved here and, perforce, had now to divert more and more attention to a battle in which infantry and artillery predominated in a vital sector: for if once a break occurred along the coast road little might be done to save those units left in the desert. On the night of October 28/29 Australians, striking north, cut two nicks out of the line near the coast in the direction of Sidi Abd el Rahman, causing 90th Light severe loss. At any moment the Germans expected this initial success to be exploited – but, strangely, nothing beyond rumours occurred. Nevertheless, partly the result of a false report of a huge Allied Force decanting onto his rear from the Qattara Depression, partly the product of despondency at news of another petrol tanker sent to the bottom, Rommel ordered the preparation of a delaying position in rear at Fuka. Of greater significance he replaced 21st Panzer opposite Kidney Ridge, with the Italian Trieste Infantry Division, and sent 21st Panzer mobile into the desert, concentrating it at last with the remnants of 15th Panzer.

But no sooner had 21st Panzer pulled back, than a furious drum-fire beating upon 90th Light announced the last phase of the battle, and sucked more German forces into the vortex on the coast, steadily achieving the uncorseting of the Italians

in the centre; these now hung flabby – vulnerable to Montgomery's body blow. For the Australian attack which disrupted 90th Light in and around Thompson's Post on the night of 30th/31st merely heralded 'Supercharge' – a far heavier stroke to be delivered two nights later in the sector left unguarded by the Germans. Indeed, the realisation that the Germans had removed the bones from the Italian corset and shifted north, prompted Montgomery to regroup and attack further south in order to concentrate on the Italians, even though it meant delaying 'Supercharge' by 24 hours.

A furious fight lasting two days now erupted where the Australians had cut the coast road on the 31st, a fight which drew in more and more German units. Thus when British infantry broke out to the south of this storm centre on the night of

November 1/2, and thrust two of their armoured divisions across the Rahman track, Afrika Korps was caught off balance - though not flat-footed. A great tank battle now blazed in the neighbourhood of Tell el Aqqaqir - the British armour under orders to fight its way out, regardless of loss, the German anti-tank gunners desperate to contain them, since to fail would throw the conflict into a mobile phase which they could not sustain.

In fact, even before the principal armoured forces clashed, British armoured cars had broken loose round the tail of the infantry assault and raided deep amongst the soft vehicles in Afrika Korps' rear, while the head-on collision at the front decimated the German armour. Disparity in tank losses almost ceased to matter, for even though one British armoured brigade lost 70 out of 94 by nightfall on the 2nd,

The 88 in peril. At El Alamein the 75 mm gun on the Sherman tank began to master this key Afrika Korps weapon

several hundred with fresh crews remained ready to sweep aside 35 exhausted German machines.

The moment had come, as Rommel realised, to race back to the Fuka line; maybe for the non-motorised Italians huddled in the original front line it was already too late – further delay certainly made it so. Signalling his decision to Hitler on the 2nd and simultaneously starting the first echelons on their journey to Fuka, Rommel re-embarked on the mobile type of warfare most suited to his temperament. Von Thoma, imposing a tenuous hold on the front with Afrika Korps – the only sort of hard hitting force that could screen a withdrawal – held the key to the escape of Panzerarmee.

Unfortunately Hitler chose this moment to send a message of exhortation, telling Rommel to hold to the last – victory or death. Arriving on the 3rd after Rommel's signal (and subject to further delay for decoding) it seemed to Rommel, at first sight, to be the answer to his message of the 2nd – a straight refusal of permission to withdraw. Rommel elected to obey, but thereby relinquished control of the withdrawal at its most critical stage, for troops left in the weakened line were told to hold on, while those already retiring to Fuka had, in some cases, to return to the wavering front.

Emotions veered and snapped at that moment. Militarily Hitler's order, if faithfully obeyed, sentenced Afrika Korps to destruction; psychologically overridden in the field for the first time by Hitler, Rommel lost faith in his Fuhrer; but by the same token the German soldiers seemed to take fresh heart and braced themselves to a desperate defence – a staunchness in ex-

Sd Kfz 231

Africa Korps depended upon motor-cycles and armoured cars as the prime movers of its reconnaissance units. Of the latter there were three basic types – four, six or eight wheeled – the latter by far the clumsiest and most easily spotted but with the best cross-country performance. In parts of the desert, armoured cars could perform as well or even better than tanks, but on steep inclines and in soft sand they were at a severe disadvantage while their limited size restricted the size of armament carried. Weight: 8 tons. Speed: 50MPH. Armour (max); 18 mm. Crew: 4. Armament: 1 x 20 mm gun, 1 x 7·9 mm mg

treme adversity which never deserted Afrika Korps.

Panzerarmee held three positions on the 3rd, none of them viable. At Fuka advanced parties of 90th Light with some scattered Italian units held a thin lay-back position, wide open to outflanking. At Alamein the original front contained a few unbroken elements of 164th Division and the Ramcke Parachute Brigade along with Italian

Victor and vanquished! General Montgomery commanding the British Eighth Army meets the captured commander of Afrika Korps, General von Thoma

infantry formations, all in full flight or supinely awaiting collection by the British. West of the Rahman Track Afrika Korps with a remnant of 'Ariete' and 90th Light prepared their immolation at Hitler's wish. And all around, the British tried both to drive further into the desert to curl round the flank of Afrika Korps, and to pierce its centre. Indeed, by the morning of November 4, the Panzerarmee, less the tiny detachment at Fuka, should have been on the point of surrender. However the breakout by major British forces which ought to have taken place on the afternoon of the 3rd fell flat, partly because of appalling confusion in the minefield gaps and bad going, but not least because of the presence of Afrika Korps fighting for prestige to its last gasp.

Astonished at being free on the morning of the 4th, Rommel asked Hitler once more for permission to withdraw – bit by bit – to Fuka, and that evening, at last, got a release. But by then 'Ariete' and most of the other Italian formations had ceased to exist, Afrika Korps was breaking up and von Thoma, fighting in a tank at its head, had been captured. A bit by bit withdrawal now lost meaning, for once on the move nothing could stop the survivors. Through the night of the 4th they raced westwards, moving mostly in the desert away from the perils of the coastal road rather in the manner practised by 1st British Armoured Division three months before.

All around, the most unutterable chaos cast friend and foe to confusion. Here and there hostile columns bumped into each other, but on a very dark night the Germans made better progress than the British, arriving in the Fuka position slightly ahead of their pursuers. Thereupon those Italians already present took off rapidly westward, leaving Rommel to do the best he could to organise a defence before the enemy main body caught up again. A rough count showed how hapless was his position – about 40 tanks, no 88s and a score or more of field and anti-tank guns along with just over a thousand infantry. To the east other comrades – notably the Ramcke Parachute Brigade – had started a long march back but their position and condition remained a mystery.

As usual, fuel ran low, water was short and the men exhausted. Day and night the aerial bombardment interfered. However, not until mid day on November 5 did the actual pursuit bother Afrika Korps, and by then the brief respite had enabled Rommel to assert some measure of control over what had nearly become a complete rout.

One answer to a minefield – a British flail tank beating its way through. The metal bobs were intended to detonate the mines when they struck. But the most effective, though slower method, was by parties of men lifting the mines by hand

Straight back

A force in withdrawal usually chooses naturally strong positions upon which to delay the pursuit in order to give time for the main body to make its escape, to evacuate essential stores and to prepare a main position in rear. Delaying positions normally rest on some sort of topographical feature, and in the Western Desert, these positions are found near the coast – at Matrûh, Halfaya, Agheila and so on – with each depending for safety upon the desert flank being kept secure by the presence of an armoured mobile force. On November 5 Panzerarmee possessed neither the strength to hold a feature nor the armoured force to cover its flank, even against an enemy a quarter the size of Eighth Army. Speed – its surviving asset – alone could save it in association with tight traffic control.

As an army contracts onto its base it becomes cluttered by its administrative units. These have to be sent back before the rearguard can give ground, while simultaneously, other fighting echelons have to be pushed further to the rear to prepare succeeding lines of resistance. In the case of Panzerarmee, the fuel shortage enforced the thinning of the forward area. On November 6 only sufficient fuel to replenish 15th Panzer between Fuka and Mersa Matrûh remained, and so 21st Panzer became stranded and had to fight 7th Armoured Division where it stood – with catastrophic results. Only four tanks out of 30 it had recovered from Alamein, got back.

To Bayerlein, in command of Afrika Korps once more, delaying actions became

ever less feasible. The Reconnaissance Unit Voss assumed an early warning role with patrols spread across the desert: what remained of Afrika Korps and 90th Light provided a mobile reserve for use in extreme emergencies, and the rest just kept going towards El Agheila, in the hope that heavy rain now falling in the desert might bog down the British. This it did – causing a total hold-up on the 7th, aggravated by fuel shortage because the British supply columns had been loaded with too much ammunition and not enough petrol. Even the Ramcke Parachutists, heartily disgruntled at being left without transport, turned up in the lorries of a British column which they had ambushed, and gradually Panzerarmee fattened as it fell back, picking up survivors and absorbing reserves, feeling somewhat happier in the knowledge that petrol had been landed at Benghazi. Leaving Mersa Matrûh on the 7th, Afrika Korps set out for Halfaya in the hope that there, perhaps, a slightly longer delay might be granted, since at last the rearguards suffered less hindrance at each stop line.

But that day Rommel received warning of an impending landing from the sea in his rear – perhaps between Tobruk and Benghazi – and on the 8th came news of something far worse – a vast invasion of the whole North African shore from Casablanca to Algiers. 'This', wrote Rommel, 'spelt the end of the army in Africa'. Soon the Allies might be in Tunisia, then Tripoli – and then there would be no escape.

To remain at Halfaya became out of the

question. Next stop must be El Agheila and even that only an intermediary one on the way to Tunisia, whence the focus shifted, 2,000 miles off: indeed, there seemed no good reason to stay in Africa at all, since, inevitably, the Anglo-Americans must obliterate whatever forces the Axis could throw across from Italy. All of a sudden the rosy hopes of victory, which had bloomed so fair in July, withered away – and not only hopes of victory in North Africa. In Russia too a menacing resistance had sprouted, for having driven easily into the Caucasus, the victorious German advance now stalled before Grozny, while at Stalingrad the Sixth Army ground itself to pulp in a mincing machine.

What Rommel most feared now came to pass in the desert – the assertion by the enemy of tactical equality hand-in-glove with technical superiority. His rearguard learned to respect the high-domed Sherman tanks with their ability to shell the anti-tank guns from out of range without exposing themselves, while the old hands fighting across the familiar Cyrenaican battlefields bemoaned the clumsiness of fresh troops who lost local engagements as the result of inferior tactics.

Not long after evacuating Halfaya on November 11, the main body of Afrika Korps out-paced Eighth Army, relegating the desert race to Agheila into an affair of light armoured vedettes. On November 13 Tobruk fell and a week later Benghazi, too, amidst a turmoil of panicky demolition measures. Meanwhile fresh German forces – in a volume that might have made all the

difference to Afrika Korps had they been sent in June – were being brought by air and sea into Tunisia to hold open a bridgehead in which Panzerarmee might seek shelter. Before El Agheila temporary lines of defence arose – one near Agedabia, a second between the sea and marshes at Mersa Brega and the third at Agheila itself. By November 23 Afrika Korps had returned to its starting point.

Afrika Korps' arrival at El Agheila, with numerous vehicles on tow, marked a turning point. Its discipline stayed exemplary; like a rock it withstood the shocks which shattered the Italians. But the loss of Benghazi made replenishment far more shaky, and with Tripoli 500 miles off and the single coastal road under constant attack, Afrika Korps lived from hand to mouth. In any case, the El Agheila position (which had never yet been seriously tested from the east) offered only temporary shelter, mainly because it could so easily be outflanked, though needless to say, Hitler ordained that it should be held, on the grounds that further retreat would undermine morale – despite the fact that the annihilation of Panzerarmee would nullify his reasons for entering Tunisia, for it would leave the southern part of Tunisia like a flask with its bottom knocked out.

There was no doubt in Rommel's mind that he must retire in haste to the Mareth Line, where it sealed off the southern approaches to Tunisia, for clearly Montgomery had stopped only in order to accumulate sufficient supplies to carry him on to Tripoli. At Mareth, with forces intact,

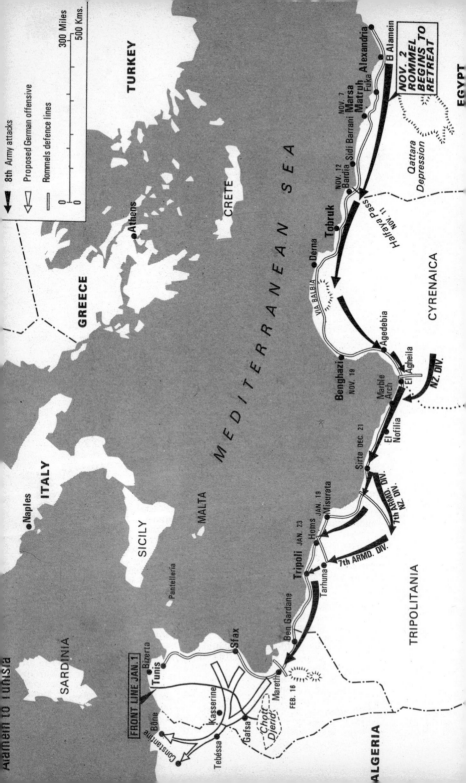

Alamein to Tunisia

TURKEY

GREECE

Athens

CRETE

ITALY

Naples

SARDINIA

SICILY

Pantelleria

MALTA

MEDITERRANEAN SEA

8th Army attacks
Proposed German offensive
Rommels defence lines

300 Miles
500 Kms.
0
0

Bizerta
Tunis
Bône
Constantine
Kasserine
Tébessa
Gafsa
Mareth
FEB. 16
Chott Djerid
Sfax
Ben Gardane
Tarhuna
FRONT LINE JAN. 1

ALGERIA

TRIPOLITANIA

7th ARMD. DIV.

Tripoli JAN. 23
Homs
Misurata JAN. 19
7th ARMD. DIV.
NZ. DIV.
Sirte DEC. 21
El Nofilia
El Agheila
Marble Arch
NZ. DIV.
Benghazi
NOV. 19
Agedebia
VIA BALBIA
Derna
Tobruk

CYRENAICA

Halfaya Pass
NOV. 11
Bardia NOV. 12
Sidi Barrani
Marsa Matruh
Fuka
NOV. 7
Alexandria
El Alamein

Qattara Depression

EGYPT

NOV. 2 ROMMEL BEGINS TO RETREAT

Fatigue in retreat. The faces of this German tank crew bear the signs of depression

Rommel stood a chance of conducting a protracted defence, although between there and Agheila certain positions at Buerat and Tarhuna might offer momentary respite. So far as Afrika Korps was concerned, the devious negotiations between their General and the Higher Commands stayed hidden, although rumours of the resources being poured into Tunisia raised sardonic comment. Had they known that Hitler and Mussolini elected to hold El Agheila purely for political reasons, regardless of the inevitable sacrifice of Afrika Korps, their reaction might have taken a different form.

In the event, Rommel outwitted the politicians, in the perilous fashion of old, at the last minute. On December 11, Eighth Army pushed towards Mersa Brega and sent a strong mobile force far round the desert flank – its goal Marble Arch, in Afrika Korps' rear. Already the unmotorised Italian infantry divisions had been sent back (despite the Dictators' standstill instruction) and so mobile forces alone comprised the defence. In good time, air reconnaissance reported the approach of the hook towards Marble Arch, the signal, regardless of contrary orders, for Afrika Korps, two Italian armoured divisions, and 90th Light to set off again, making for Buerat.

It turned into an extraordinary journey. Quite regardless of tactical demands, the retiring Axis formations had to calculate every move in relation to each litre of petrol. Halts were conditioned more by fuel shortage than tactical necessity, though often it would have been better to withdraw earlier or counter-attack sooner to relieve some dreadful crisis. Consequently each late departure became fraught with peril, unnecessarily costly in men and machines, and frequently terrifying during the last minute run of the gauntlet, past British armour and guns crowding in from the open desert to block defiles in the rear. The ceaseless bombing merely boosted the impending confusion, and the fact that the bulk of the fugitives arrived at Buerat while the British 'mopped up' an empty pocket close to Nofilia, owed as much to good luck and strong nerves as to proper organisation.

Afrika Korps' future now depended upon Rommel's ability to circumvent the do-or-die standstill orders. Here he was aided by the Italians and by General Montgomery, for the former had orders to stand and fight, but could be prevailed upon to withdraw at the threat of being left behind as at Alamein: while the latter, in his determination to maintain an overwhelming force in case Afrika Korps riposted, worried about overtaxing his supply resources to an extent that would have given Rommel cause for envy. Had he but half Montgomery's resources . . . ?

Afrika Korps' role in the retreat to Buerat (where it arrived on December 26) took second place to remaining intact, and 15th Panzer, intent on eating Christmas Dinner in Sirte, had to pack up in haste in response to reports of a British column encircling them. Twenty-first Panzer already guarding the southern flank at

Buerat, now welcomed 15th Panzer – marking a temporary re-unification of Afrika Korps – for at last the Higher Command reached the conclusion that Tripolitania could no longer be defended, and agreed that they would leave at Montgomery's pace, though hedging their temerity with a disinclination to give specific orders for the withdrawal of the non-mobile troops.

It is unlikely that the rank and file of Afrika Korps recognised the diplomatic rearguard action their C-in-C was fighting against the intransigence of the Higher Command, while they upheld the rearguard against the British. When they saw Rommel pass by, his demeanour was that of cheerful confidence – though somewhat finely drawn. Moreover the scrapes he got them into in no way damaged his prestige in their eyes since he usually pulled them through, and it encouraged them to notice how infrequently the British followed hard on their heels. Now in the light of the news from Tunisia, many of the troops at Buerat started back at once to occupy the defences near Mareth. Hence the first retrograde step to Tarhuna by the Italians and the withdrawal of 21st Panzer on January 13 to Gabes made military sense – the more so since the first hint of an Anglo-American attack from the north against Mareth had already been noticed.

The reduction of the original Afrika Korps in Tripolitania demonstrated, as nothing else could, that Rommel had forsaken all further offensive operations there, so when Eighth Army advanced again on January 15, it was to get caught amongst a sea of mines by an enemy who shot and ran, and an Afrika Korps consisting of 15th Panzer (with only 36 tanks), 90th Light, 164th Division and the Ramcke Brigade. Step by step, faster and faster went the retreat, with hardly a pause at Tarhuna, and no stop at all at Tripoli. Nevertheless, British progress paid careful respect to the sting in the tail of Afrika Korps – and advanced warily from bound to bound, ever tense for the sort of riposte which, as happened at Buerat, could suddenly kill a dozen tanks at the expense of only two German machines.

On January 22 Afrika Korps said farewell to Tripoli and turned its head to Tunisia and the Mareth Line, hoping that there a long stand might be made, for the Allied effort in Northern Tunisia had clearly expended itself against the German build-up. On paper the Mareth Line, built by the French against the Italians before the war, and founded on deep obstacles with a reputedly unturnable southern flank, promised to be a position of substance. Best of all it offered the chance of holding with infantry while the mobile troops took a rest and prepared for offensive operations.

But, to Rommel, the old French position looked badly sited and eminently vulnerable to outflanking and he preferred a stronger one to the north aligned with Wadi Akarit. But his personal position had been shaken and his health was declining. Those above him resented the manner in which he had evaded orders and executed so precipitate a retreat, and so on January 26 he learned he was to be replaced by an Italian – General Messe. At once his thoughts turned to the men. 'They were very dear to me', he wrote.

The elation of victory. A British all-arms column in the advance. Left foreground a Sherman tank, centre infantry carriers and supply vehicles, including a jeep; right foreground, 6-pounder anti-tank gun on portee mounting

The spoiling battles

German tanks in Tunisia

In many respects every offensive undertaken by Afrika Korps, except the improvised advance from Tobruk which ended in the final repulse at Alam Halfa, started as a spoiling action designed to cut back British strength before it could mature. Within the muddled framework of the Axis Tunisian strategy this policy prevailed to the end – and never more so than in their offensives radiating from southern Tunisia. To begin with, Axis Forces in Tunisia operated as two separate forces, ill co-ordinated by Commando Supremo in Rome with Marshals Kesselring and Cavallero dashing backwards and forwards in attempting to resolve the misunderstandings between field commanders and city politicians.

Panzerarmee's rearguard trailed into Tunisia on February 13, dropping a line of outposts to contain Eighth Army at Medenine, the whole force assuming responsibility for the area south of Gafsa under a new name, 1st Italian Army, with the fresh Italian commander, General Messe – an appointment in name alone, at first, since Rommel managed to delay his own departure. Of the original Afrika Korps only a weakened 15th Panzer Division remained, though the German 90th and 164th Divisions bolstered the swarm of shaken Italian formations filling the Mareth Line.

North of Gafsa, Colonel-General von Arnim's Fifth Panzer Army had stabilised its front from Faid through Fondouk and Medjez el Bab to the sea, near Cape Serrat. Von Arnim, in accord with his temperament, now planned a defensive – offensive operation against the Americans between Faid and Gafsa in order to acquire more favourable defensive positions. Of secondary importance was the destruction of forces in the Tebéssa area, although he considered it unlikely that his two panzer divisions, 10th and 21st (both quite strong in armour once the latter received rapid reinforcement) could possibly accomplish this mission.

Characteristically, Rommel took the opposite view and proposed a spoiling attack by united forces under one commander through Gafsa, to forestall the threat of American pressure on Mareth's rear. In fact, the Americans themselves felt equally vulnerable and actually undertook local withdrawals which prompted Rommel to ask von Arnim for the use of the 10th Panzer against Gafsa. But von Arnim rejected this at once because he needed 10th Panzer at Faid – an attitude so typical of the Axis command schism at this time. So, for over a week, Commando Supremo negotiated (because it could not order) in an effort to convert dispersed prods into one solid punch. Neither Rommel nor von Arnim would donate forces to help the other, since Rommel could ill afford to detach the

evacuated 15th Panzer from its post in the Mareth Line, and von Arnim saw no reason to give up his own projects in favour of somebody else's.

In the upshot, von Arnim more or less had his way and sent his deputy – General Ziegler – to command 10th and 21st Panzer in the main thrust against the 1st US Armoured Division through Faid to Sbeitla (starting on February 14, 1943) while Rommel provided a so-called Afrika Korps Assault Group under General Buelowius to operate against Gafsa in the direction of Kasserine. So weak was this detachment, however (its striking element comprising only 26 Mark III and IV tanks from 8th Panzer Regiment plus 23 M 13 Italians from the Centauro Division), that its mission could be regarded as little more than flank guard to Ziegler. But its directive proposed exploitation to Tebéssa once Ziegler could transfer 21st Panzer after completion of its initial task. On paper, at any rate, Rommel had achieved the possibility of re-unifying Afrika Korps and striking a profound strategic blow.

But neither Ziegler nor von Arnim encompassed Rommel's grand manner, although on the heels of the disaster at Stalingrad some sort of revivalist victory was needed. None dreamed, of course, that the Americans' lack of experience would bring about such a rout as struck 1st Armoured Division when 10th and 21st Panzer Divisions, converging from two directions, enveloped them. By the evening of the 17th virtually two-thirds of the American force had been eliminated, Ziegler was at the gates of Sbeitla, and Afrika Korps Assault Group, finding the Americans had pulled back from Gafsa on the night of the 14th, had set off to Thélepté in hot pursuit. This complete tactical victory at once offered the chance of a strategic decision. With the American armour destroyed and British armour in First Army in the process of re-equipping with Sherman tanks, only scratch forces could interpose between a concentrated raid deep into the rear through Tebéssa, possibly as far north as the important supply port at Bone. Nor could Eighth Army intervene in time, for the port of Tripoli had not been fully restored and the light forces at Medinine lacked strength or enough provisions for an offensive, even though Montgomery tried all he could to simulate one.

If, now, the Germans had created a unified command of their own, Afrika Korps, with 21st Panzer in the fold again – perhaps even with 10th Panzer as well – might have swept all before them. That they did not stemmed from the narrowness of von Arnim's largely defensive outlook, Ziegler's muddled tactical handling and Rommel's loss of favour with the vacillating Commando Supremo. Concentrating solely on

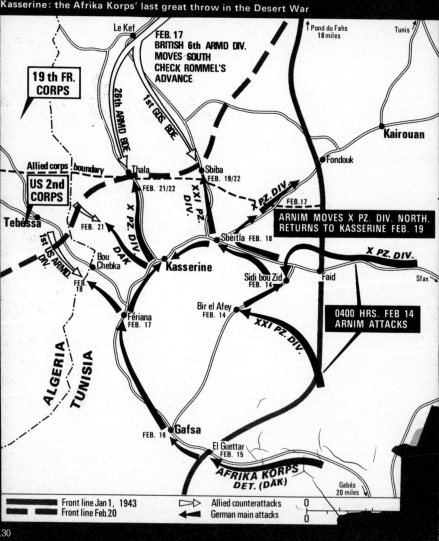

Kasserine: the Afrika Korps' last great throw in the Desert War

The Germans meet the Americans. United States Army prisoners of war march by, watched by Muslim ladies at a discreet distance

Pz Kw IV with L/48 75 mm gun

Built primarily to match the excellent Russian T34/76 tank, this improved version of Pz Kw IV was more than a match for all Allied tanks in 1942 except the Sherman. Only a small proportion of this up-gunned, up-armoured German tank made up the armoured strength of Afrika Korps, but from Alam Halfa onwards it was the backbone of its Panzer Divisions.
Weight: 23 tons. Speed: 25 MPH. Armour (max): 50 mm. Crew: 5. Armament: 1 x 75 mm gun, 2 x 7·9 mm mg

the original spoiling operation, von Arnim told Ziegler to destroy the Allied stores at Sbeitla and then to strike a local blow northwards towards Fondouk – propelling 21st Panzer into a stiff fight at Sbeitla, and sending 10th Panzer on a wild goose chase, since the Allies had already withdrawn from Fondouk.

Afrika Korps, meantime, performed with verve despite its attenuated numbers. The original gaiety took hold again, the officers and men on splendid terms when purchasing eggs from the Arabs, who welcomed them as if the Americans had imposed generations of oppression. Now American equipment and petrol replenished Axis stocks as had once the supply dumps of Eighth Army, while, at the front, green enemy units frequently abandoned unharmed vehicles; and in the rear, mountains of stores burned. To Rommel the vista of his original concept – the unified drive through Tebéssa to the north, revived, but finding on the 18th, that von Arnim would not listen, he addressed his proposal direct to Kesselring and Commando Supremo.

Rommel's erstwhile Aide de Camp, Lieutenant Schmidt, once declared that Rommel was neither a genius nor a superman – but he did possess a subtle imagination linked with a deep understanding of

the capability of Afrika Korps. Unfortunately for him, his wider unconventional perception overwhelmed both friends and opponents alike and from Halder to Kesselring, Wavell to Alexander, conjured up adventures beyond their comprehension. In the same way as Halder and Wavell could not envisage Rommel's chances of success in April 1941, neither Kesselring nor General Alexander (who now held operational command over the entire Allied effort in Tunisia under General Eisenhower) believed Rommel could pull off a deep penetration so wide of the main battlefield, as an approach through Tebéssa would take him. So Kesselring bowed to a compromise when Commando Supremo decided to allow Rommel to command two panzer divisions, but only on a short hook through Thala. Alexander, on his side, concurred, taking it for granted that this course would be adopted, and reinforced these approaches instead of those leading to Tebéssa.

Of course, nobody can say what impact Rommel's grander scheme might have achieved had he had his way and taken his old 21st Panzer along with the Afrika Korps Assault Group, backed by 10th Panzer. Possibly the psychological effect on the Anglo-American Army might have been decisive: it is possible too that they might

have been forced to withdraw into Algeria –
in which case their losses in material must
have grown enormous – and subsequent
operations by Eighth Army might either
have been precipitate and hazardous or
delayed by Montgomery's caution in the
face of a rampant opponent.

In the event, not even the short hook got
off to a proper start. Because 21st Panzer
had been committed already by Ziegler to
a lunge towards Sbiba, 10th Panzer had to
be switched to join Afrika Korps at
Kasserine and could not arrive until the
20th. Afrika Korps Assault Group, to keep

**The fruits of Kasserine Pass. A German armoured infantry carrier heads a
column consisting almost of more American vehicles than those of German
manufacture**

the Americans on the run, simply had to storm the Kasserine Pass in order to open the way to Thala for 10th Panzer – and in so doing, confirmed Alexander's judgement of where the main threat lay. But Afrika Korps failed to adjust itself to foreign terrain as, at one leap, they found themselves swept up from flat desert levels into mountain warfare where it is mandatory to seize the heights before advancing in the valleys.

Thirty-third Reconnaissance Unit took a hard look at the hills on either side of the pass on the evening of February 19 – and in the process nearly bounced the Americans out. Next day a more formal assault by two battalions of Panzer Grenadier Regiment Afrika, followed by tanks from 8th Panzer Regiment, made very heavy going, partly as a result of well-directed American artillery fire and partly because of its failure to secure the heights. By nightfall they lay short of their objective, although the American defenders hung on the verge of collapse. A similar tale could be told of 21st Panzer at Sbiba: here, too, a pass held by American and British infantry proved too stiff a task for tanks, whose every move invariably took them into the muzzles of anti-tank guns firing straight down the solitary road. Losses piled up and progress died: the right fist of Rommel's double punch had stalled.

Then at Kasserine on the 20th things looked up, for although renewed attacks that morning by German and Italian infantry got off to a slow start, a hammer blow at 1 pm by 10th Panzer Division finally broke the Americans, pounded up the road, destroying all the tanks in a British battlegroup on its way to Kasserine, and ended up that evening face-to-face with the British 26th Armoured Brigade ten miles south of the objective, Thala. Afrika Korps moved equally fast, chasing the Americans into the western hills, securing 10th Panzer's flank and mounting a threat to Tebéssa.

On both sides of the line a pessimistic tone sounded through the councils of war. The Allied commanders feared for their thin defences both at Sbiba and Thala – a fear well justified for throughout February 21, 10th Panzer stormed at 26th Armoured Brigade and pressed them relentlessly back to within three miles of Thala. At that instant, General Anderson, the Commander of British First Army, warned the defenders of Sbiba to prepare to fall back 40 miles because their position might become untenable if Thala fell.

But the lack of progress by 21st and the slowness of 10th Panzer (linked with its apparent exhaustion) preyed on Rommel's judgement. He reasoned that only quick results would gain ultimate success, while the stiff British resistance demonstrated how the advance was running straight into

The land of Tunisia. Kasserine Pass. A great change from the open desert

Rommel talks to his men. Even in defeat their intent expressions portray a lasting confidence

137

the enemy reserves – as he always feared it would. In fact, at dusk, the leading German tanks following on the heels of a retirement by 26th Armoured Brigade, burst undetected into the midst of the main British blocking position and proceeded to set about the defenders at close range. All night a pitched battle raged while, in the British rear, the arrival of three American artillery battalions introduced a fresh, and as it turned out, decisive element. For when these guns opened fire at dawn, the Germans took it for a counter-attack and stood fast instead of pressing on, as well they might, and at mid-day on the 22nd, both sides still sat back in doubt. Meanwhile 21st Panzer merely glowered at Sbiba while Afrika Korps rebounded impotently from the improvised American hill defences to the west.

But the Germans could not afford to stand still – the more so since the poor weather, which up till then had curtailed flying, began to improve. Rommel, meeting Kesselring at Kasserine that afternoon, had to decide to get on or get out, and in the circumstances – bearing in mind the latent air threat and the fact that the objective of the offensive was not of his choosing – his selection of the second course comes as no surprise. Its masterly execution, however, excited admiration even from the enemy, for, in the first place, neither the British nor the Americans realised at once that their assailants had departed, and then, as they followed up and found the way strewn with the most ingenious barrier of demolitions and booby traps, it drew from Eisenhower the appreciation of 'virtually a new weapon in warfare'.

Within five days the front ran roughly where it had been on the 14th. But on the Axis side a new appointment, Commander Army Group 'Afrika', had been conferred upon Rommel – restoring him to favour and placing him in full charge from February 24, of von Arnim's Fifth Panzer and Messe's First Italian Army. In a way this represented an extraordinary choice, for Kesselring had noticed at Kasserine that Rommel appeared mentally and physically exhausted. Nevertheless, Rommel could at last combine the whole Axis armoured force as he wished, as one offensive unit under the control of its most polished instrument – Afrika Korps.

The reorganisation. came too late to avert one last piecemeal act – von Arnim's imminent attack against Medjez el Bab on February 26, using the best part of 10th and 21st Panzer. This prohibited a lightning switch against Eighth Army, although there is little doubt that if 10th, 15th and 21st Panzer Divisions had been thrown against Medenine immediately after the Kasserine withdrawal, significant results m i g h t h a v e b e e n a c h i e v e d. F o r Montgomery's enforced premature offen-

sive to distract German attention from the Kasserine area now left him weak and in no fit state to prosecute a stiff defence. In fact, on February 27, only one infantry division backed by 7th Armoured Division held the line from the coast inland to the outskirts of Medenine, and not until March 4 could an extra reinforced infantry division, plus an armoured brigade, be brought up. Between those dates Eighth Army lay vulnerable. But subsequently, in the midst of planning an assault on the Mareth Line, Montgomery let it be known that an attack by Afrika Korps at Medenine would be as fully welcome as had been the attack at Alam Halfa.

On Rommel's part, the concentration of the three panzer divisions under Afrika Korps, for an attack whose objective he announced. as 'Tripoli', bore no resemblance to the situation on August 31, 1942 at Alam Halfa. Then he strove for a knock-out blow: now he merely bargained for delay. There was no time to carry out a sweep round the south of the British position, so the approach had to be direct, along separate routes, 15th Panzer crossing the open plain from Mareth, 21st debouching from the high ground past Toujane and 10th struggling down the track from Hallouf; all three directed at Medenine in the rear of the British line and, thereby striking the defence separated in space and, in the event, in time as well.

Afrika Korps, potent as a team once more with a combined strength of 140 tanks, nevertheless felt aware that the task ahead might be its toughest yet. Very little was known of the British infantry, the positions of the minefields or of most of the 500 odd anti-tank guns. Nor was it known that amongst those guns waited the new 17-pounder or exactly where the armoured reserve stood ready.

To the British, the German intentions came as no surprise. There had been a brush with 15th Panzer on March 3 and throughout the 4th and 5th air reconnaissance had detected the approach of the three columns (although attempts to penetrate the screen of German reconnaissance units invariably failed). Fog shrouded the front early on the 6th, but did not prevent the Luftwaffe and artillery pummelling the British front, even though it obscured the preliminary German moves.

Then at 9 am the panzers came into view and the attack spread along the front with its centre of gravity to the north of Medenine. Puzzled by the stillness within the defenders' lines (as many an attacker of the British has been over the centuries from the days of the English bowmen) the panzers came within 400 yards before a howling artillery barrage struck them and the banks of anti-tank guns threw off their camouflage to come into action. Only 15th Panzer pushed its attack right home

Medium artillery of Afrika Korps passes a burning allied supply vehicle

The Panzer Divisions drive into the hills

The Mareth Line – view from a pill-box
giving an impression of the fields of
fire incorporated in this French-built
defensive system

suffering proportionate losses, while 21st Panzer blundered indecisively, and 10th seemed disinclined to come to grips.

By mid-day the wind had been taken out of the first German rush; neither HQ Afrika Korps under General Cramer nor Messe's First Italian Army, nor even Rommel himself from where he stood over-looking the scene up by Hallouf, seemed anxious to take a grasp on the proceedings. Meanwhile the British disdained to commit their armour. Perhaps each German commander, so used to Rommel bustling in their midst, awaited his traditional intervention; perhaps Afrika Korps had lost its bite for ever. Certainly Rommel looked and acted like a badly sick man – the jaundice and desert sores erasing the keen look from his face.

In the event, the three German divisional commanders seem to have co-ordinated the next attempt amongst themselves so that their second attack launched in the afternoon put the infantry in the lead behind an artillery and aerial bombard-ment with the tanks following. But again a curtain of artillery fire obliterated the attackers who nowhere got within small-arms range. No Afrika Korps offensive had ever received such a savage rebuff. The portent seemed obvious.

And as the Germans drew off in confusion that evening, nobody read the omens more clearly than Rommel himself. Fifty tanks had been left behind, leaving barely a hundred to compete in future with 400 enemy or more. Medenine was Afrika Korps' last great offensive and Rommel's swan song. A few days later von Arnim took over Army Group Afrika and the sick man returned to Europe for ever, leaving the situation perhaps more desperate even than he had found it.

The Wadi Zigzaou is a deep, natural trench running 22 miles inland from the Mediterranean to the Matmata Hills. As such it is a formidable tank obstacle and the foundation of the Mareth Line. The waterless Matmata Hills are also a rugged barrier and became doubly so with their few tracks mined, blocked and held even by only light forces. But a stretch of open desert, – the Dahar – almost devoid of tracks, which lay to the west of the Matmata range thence leading through a narrow pass – the Tebaga Gap – towards El

Infantry awaits the word to retreat

142

Hamma and Gabes, opened an avenue pointing deep into the open flank and rear of the Mareth Line. Prewar, the French had dismissed the Dahar as impassable to a mechanised force. Rommel in 1943 doubted their judgement and Montgomery had evidence that a way round was feasible.

Already relays of British Long Range Desert Group patrols had penetrated through Wilder's Gap, past Tebaga and right into the El Hamma Plain. They were followed by a more substantial French column which, under General Leclerc, had come to Tripoli from French Equatorial Africa: in March it occupied a Dahar base at Ksar Rhilane. Tender in this area, Messe sent German reconnaissance units, backed by Stukas, to dig out Leclerc's wasps' nest on March 10 – and recoiled with heavy German losses. From then on the probability that a flanking attack might come through the Dahar rarely strayed far from First Italian Army's calculations, forcing them to deploy to check both that and the Mareth Line approaches.

Screened by outposts – notably on a feature called Horseshoe – Wadi Zigzaou's defence for most of its length fell to Italians,

corsetted in the fashionable manner by German detachments, ribbed by 90th Light holding the centre sector and 164th Light in the Matmata Hills. Earmarked for immediate counter-attack, 15th Panzer (with only 50 tanks) hid five miles behind the wadi. In the Tebaga Gap an amorphous collection of Italian frontier guards mixed with Libyan garrison troops under General Mannerini, called the Sahara Group, tentatively aligned itself along an old Roman Wall, frightfully short of the confidence of the legionnaires of old. Afrika Korps as usual played the leading role with 10th Panzer watching the Americans at Gafsa, and 21st Panzer in General Reserve at Gabes poised to intervene either at Mareth or Gafsa. Thus Afrika Korps acted as Army Group Reserve, its HQ a sort of clearing house for von Arnim's priorities.

Now that Rommel had gone the relationships between Italian and German within First Italian Army took a turn for the worse. General Bayerlein, appointed as German Liaison Officer to Messe (despite his self-advertised mistrust of Italians), immediately assumed direct control over all German troops, pressing the Italians into

A fuel cache

On the defensive – a German gun crew watches for its fall of shot

On the run – the car in the foreground
has been run over by a tank

conforming to German wishes whether they liked it or not. A virus that emphasised national self-preservation before team spirit gathered strength and percolated deeper into the arteries of the Tunisian defence.

But the British plan was simple and clearly the product of one brain – Montgomery's. First the Mareth Line covering positions must be driven in on March 16 and 17. Then on the night of the 20th the Wadi Zigzaou was to be crossed near its mouth, to allow strong infantry and armoured forces to collect on the other side prior to engaging man-to-man, tank against tank in the familiar Alamein pattern. As a subsidiary, albeit powerful operation, the 2nd New Zealand Division with an armoured brigade was to move secretly through Wilder's Gap, join Leclerc and attempt a surprise penetration of the Tebaga Gap just as the main attack on the Wadi reached its climax.

Once again the Desert Air Forces would fly in strength, joined by the US Air Force from Tunisia, just as the IInd US Corps, recovering from its setback, would begin a push towards Gabes. More than ever now the Luftwaffe suffered eclipse. Axis information now lacked body and clarity and events revealed themselves all too often at only short notice. Even so their soldiers hardly lost a trick; the preliminary Mareth operation in failing to clear the Horseshoe, proving particularly costly to the British and a fillip to the defenders, 90th Light. Messe and Bayerlein now took it for granted that a full blooded breaching operation would aim to cross Wadi Zigzaou – and reinforced the haunches of the actual place with a battalion of German infantry. But at first no confirmation of their suspicions concerning a major move through the Dahar came to hand and so they took no positive steps to reinforce the Tebaga Gap until the 20th.

That morning, however, the New Zealanders, moving only by night to reach Ksar Rhilane, received a message from General Montgomery stating (on somewhat uncertain authority) that the enemy knew of their whereabouts. Hearing this, the New Zealanders threw concealment aside and pressed on in daylight – coming into sight of the Tebaga Gap that evening. But the terrific flurry exposed their intentions as nothing else could, and possibly as Montgomery intended. A warning from Messe to 164th Light Division to quit the Matmata Hills and fill the Tebaga Gap engineered, if slowly, the desired reaction, but even so, the New Zealanders might easily have broken through Sahara Group's thin wall next morning with untold impact – for by then all eyes focussed on Wadi Zigzaou.

At 8.30 pm on March 20 a characteristic British artillery barrage crashed down on the Italian Young Fascists near the coast, to be followed in swift succession by infantry fanning out to seize the bridgehead, behind which crossings for tanks and guns could be constructed. By daybreak, after intense fighting, the bridgehead coalesced, but then the water-logged wadi-bed loosened, permitting only four British tanks and a handful of anti-tank guns to cross that night. In fact this lack of progress actually aided the British, for so little were Messe and Bayerlein impressed that they withheld a counter-attack in the belief that this bridgehead might only be a diversion. Had 15th Panzer gone in then it could have annihilated the British toehold, but they just watched and poured down high explosive upon the crossing place until the morning of the 22nd. Then, after a second night in which the British widened their bridgehead and dragged 40 tanks across, there could no longer be any doubt that this was the main assault.

Quite by chance, 15th Panzer timed its stroke to perfection, leaving cover just as a heavy downpour of rain grounded the British air force and obstructed observation by their artillery. Heavily outgunned, the British Valentine tanks lost two-thirds of their strength in a fighting withdrawal to the wadi's edge, but by nightfall, with the bridgehead covered in smoke and dust and the British infantry exhausted, there could be no argument that the main British assault had failed. Fifteenth Panzer pulled back into reserve. Eighth Army reverted to the defensive.

Interest now switched to the Matmata Hills and the Tebaga Gap where, on the 21st, a cloying inertia gripped the New Zealanders who watched Sahara Group fire a lot of ammunition to no great effect while they prepared their own deliberate assault for the night 21st/22nd – an attack which achieved its objective in next to no time. Sahara Group disintegrated, the way ahead lay open and the armour could have broken through. Why, then, did it not do so? General Freyberg's fears that, by thrusting ahead, he would be exposed to the full blast of Afrika Korps and Rommel (not knowing that he no longer commanded) provided the answer; of such is the value of reputation! On the 22nd therefore – and, indeed, for four days following, a stalemate settled on both fronts. Montgomery withdrew across the Wadi Zigzaou, while 164th Light and 21st Panzer arrived at Tebaga to make faces at the New Zealanders.

At the moment of failure Montgomery boldly shifted his centre of gravity, sending 4th Indian Infantry Division clambering amongst the hills on a short hook onto the Mareth Line near Beni Zelten, and a fresh armoured division, the 1st, through Wilder's Gap to join the New Zealanders. Before its arrival late on the afternoon of the 26th, the affair at Tebaga had resolved itself into

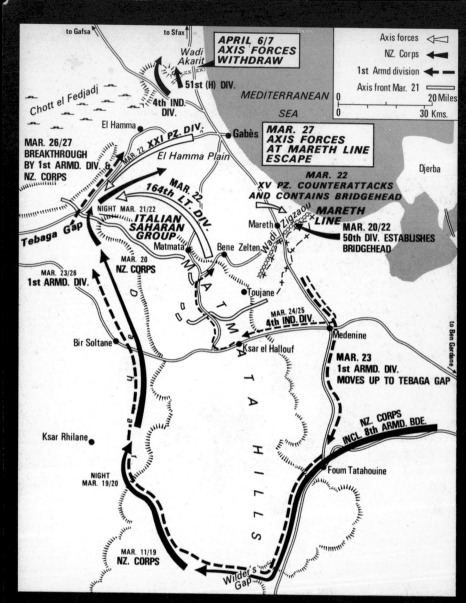

Mareth: Montgomery's 'left hook' forces the Afrika Korps to retreat again

Old adversary Pz Kw III with a dead crew member rests at Mareth. Notice the use of extra track plates to reinforce the armour

New enemy weapons – a 15 cm Nebelwerfer after its first appearance against the Allies

a gun duel aimed at the slow elimination of German positions overlooking the Roman Wall, though on the 25th, Kesselring visited the area, concluded that 164th Light stood in no great danger, and even tried to provoke Messe into a counter-offensive.

But von Arnim took a longer view, coloured by the spectre of an American attack through Maknassy to cut off 1st Italian Army once and for all. In a typically sterile debate he succeeded in persuading or overruling all concerned into a withdrawal to the Wadi Akarit, north of the El Hamma Plain, to begin, as was usual, with the removal of the unmotorised Italian formations – on the night of March 25/26.

Throughout the 26th, except for a temporary lull imposed by a sandstorm blowing across their airfields, the Allied air forces pounded the Axis airfields and then, half an hour prior to the land assault, unleashed waves of fighter-bombers against the German troops blocking the exits from the Tebaga Gap. As no other such attack had ever done before, this one paralysed and isolated the front, smashing guns and equipment, cutting communications and pinning down the Afrika Korps' formations. Then, catching the Germans in a daze, British armour and mechanised infantry, following a rolling artillery barrage, engulfed them; by nightfall the line had broken in pieces – with 21st Panzer brushed aside and the British 1st Armoured Division rolling headlong towards El Hamma.

Lesser armies would have cracked, and that night panic could so easily have set in on a grand scale at HQ, as a deluge of confused reports came in of gun-posts overrun and units decimated. By moonlight the British tanks were going strong, hastening the flight of every Axis unit in Southern Tunisia, and the Italians were racing back to Wadi Akarit from Mareth, their rearguard, once more, the faithful 90th Light. Into the approaches of El Hamma drove a few German anti-tank guns, scraped up from outlying detachments as a rallying point for the fragments which had evaded the avalanche at Tebaga. At El Guettar, where IInd US Corps pressed in on 10th Panzer, Afrika Korps fought skilfully but desperately to keep safe the flank and rear of the Wadi Akarit position in order that its old comrades in the south might escape.

It is a key to the success of an armoured breakthrough that it must keep rolling in order to prevent the enemy consolidating. This, in the face of innumerable dogged German rearguards, the British failed to do, – so, although they could claim the destruction and capture of great enemy resources, mostly Italian, it had to be admitted that the main enemy mobile spring – Afrika Korps – had once more struggled free.

But Afrika Korps no longer maintained an offensive capability. The one counter-attack mounted by 15th Panzer with its surviving ten tanks against the New Zealanders near El Hamma failed so ignominiously that the New Zealanders did not even realise it had come and gone. Greater significance became attached to operations against the Americans close to the Maknassy Pass.

The Germans did not hold much respect for the American contingent and so the cautious twin advance by Patton's IInd US Corps to Maknassy and El Guettar were calmly contained to cover preparations for a counter stroke at an appropriate moment – at the height of the Mareth Line defence. On the night of March 22/23 the Americans seemed to be on the point of breaking through the Maknassy Pass, while other spearheads rode east from El Guettar in the neighbourhood of Bou Hamran. At the Maknassy Pass, the Axis garrison had actually begun to pull out when, in typically aggressive style, Rommel's old personal escort arrived under Colonel Lang, took in the situation at a glance, stabilised it with a few sharp, local skirmishes and safely kept control of this important feature. Much credit belongs to Group Lang for wresting the initiative from the Americans – but the principal cause for a cessation of pressure at Maknassy could be found, in fact, near El Guettar.

Here 10th Panzer, concentrating secretly from reserve on the night of March 22/23, swept violently out of the hills, watched by Cramer from the heights, to catch 1st US Infantry Division on the march in the low ground below. The surprise, density and momentum of the foray carried all before it, carving right through to the artillery lines until checked by a hastily-laid minefield. Pausing to re-organise and recover damaged tanks, 10th Panzer jumped off again in the evening, utterly confident in its superiority over a hesitant opponent.

And then it happened – but let 18th US Combat Team describe it:

'Troops started to appear from all directions, mostly from tanks. Hit Anti-Tank Company and 3rd Battalion. Our artillery crucified them with high explosive shells and they were falling like flies. Tanks seem to be moving to the rear; those that could move'.

The German attack died. No longer could Afrika Korps treat the Americans with disdain, try though the Axis High Command might to foster this impression.

The wounded. Perhaps with a ticket to the Fatherland

In the line

First Italian Army lay in the bottom of a rather threadbare sack at Wadi Akarit where it dug in and received the last of the German rearguard on March 29. Fortunately the follow-up by Eighth Army had been tardy, but on the other hand, the Italian troops had virtually stopped fighting, 164th Light practically ceased to exist, and 15th and 21st Panzer Divisions owned just a handful of tanks, whilst their battlegroups were seriously mixed up in the turmoil of the rearguard. Only 90th Light, which had been least heavily involved, retained a semblance of good order. Thus the two Italian corps detailed to block the formidable, but somewhat shallow, Akarit bottleneck, could only line the front with an array of truncated units and a few strong German fibres – but precious little in the way of a mobile reserve: just 22 tanks in 15th Panzer on April 6. Therefore a position that lacked depth also lacked the reserve so essential to its lasting security.

Afrika Korps had no part in the static defence at Wadi Akarit, even though one of its old components did. Instead, with 10th and 21st Panzer, it played cat and mouse against General Patton's resurgent IInd US Corps, staving off the landslide at Maknassy and El Guettar. But the insistent rumbling from that direction throughout the Mareth battle introduced restraint into each commitment of the Axis General Reserve, and acted as the telling factor in persuading von Arnim to pull back to Akarit. Moreover, the tentative rate of the American advance seemed to

hint at something more sinister, for although the Germans were not to know that General Alexander had prohibited an advance beyond the line Maknassy – Faid – Fondouk, the threat of a sudden breakthrough to the sea behind Akarit could never be forgotten. So innumerable threats hung over the Axis flank, demanding the presence of every mobile element that could be scraped together.

The pronouncements of the Axis commanders, from von Arnim downwards, now adopted a characteristically Rommel tone. The old cries for equipment and fuel interspersed with requests for total withdrawal to the mainland (a political impossibility) or instructions on methods of arranging a surrender, beat ever louder on the eardrums of Hitler, Mussolini and their advisers. And, of course, the usual demands for resistance to the death echoed back. But of the defences at Akarit, von Arnim reported that they were 'nothing special' and would be given up in the enemy's good time – not that of First Italian Army.

Eighth Army selected April 6 as the time: its method, a direct assault, since salt marshes covered the western flank and the sea the eastern one. Extended beyond the Wadi, itself a tank obstacle, a ditch filled the gaps between high, dominating ground, while minefields barred the approaches to the ditch. Without exception, the prominent hills, Djebel Fatnassa in the west and Djebel Roumana in the centre, held the key to the breaching of the wadi and the ditches. The method of attack therefore offered few alternatives and, in the event,

Signs of disruption. German and Italian prisoners
after the battle of the Mareth Line

the only surprise inflicted on General Messe came with its timing. Most of Montgomery's formal assaults had come on moonlit nights – but with the moon out of phase no need for haste in retiring to the ramparts of the ultimate Tunisian bridgehead at Enfidaville seemed necessary.

Messe intended to make the British pay dearly for crossing the ditch. But Fatnassa fell in one night, on April 6, to the men of the mountain-trained 4th Indian Division, exposing the Wadi Akarit position to outflanking without the strength to counterattack to put matters right. At daybreak a full blown two divisional assault, behind a wall of high explosive, was flung across both ditches and up Roumana itself and at once almost the entire front went up in flames.

Italians surrendered at call while the Germans fought on, watched anxiously by Generals von Arnim, Messe, Cramer (of Afrika Korps) and Bayerlein from Messe's Headquarters: theirs merely to decide when the last reserve had been expended, how soon the break might come, and how quickly the whole of First Italian Army should be raced back to Enfidaville. Already Cramer had pulled 80 tanks from El Guettar into reserve behind Akarit – their removal from the face of the American advance releasing new pressures upon Akarit's rear. By mid-day, 90th Light had been thrown against Roumana but, after initial success, wrestled in deadlock on the crest. Eastward, 15th Panzer fought until exhausted while forty of Afrika Korps' tanks failed in a somewhat feeble attempt close to Fatnassa.

In point of fact, the will to fight had partially deserted the higher command, many of whose prominent members spent the afternoon in heaping recriminations on the Italians and disagreeing amongst themselves about what to do next. Each knew his own mind but none cared much for the ideas of the others. All around, the enemy air force strafed everything that moved, holding Afrika Korps' counterattack almost without assistance from ground troops – an action which finally convinced von Arnim that Akarit could no longer hold out and that everybody must bolt that night at top speed for Enfidaville. Indeed the decision came not a moment too soon, for with the entire mobile reserve struggling like rabbits in the bottom of the sack, General Alexander planned to tie its neck. Maknassy had been given up on the 22nd, but Afrika Korps had continued to hold the hills to the east, absorbing the Americans' attentions. However, the IXth Corps (of 1st British Army) stood in General Reserve around Sbiba, ready for a swift stroke, to cut the Axis rear near Kairouan. With so many different corps and so many air forces converging on the hapless First Italian Army in the open country south of Enfidaville, the difficulty would soon

become one of telling friend from foe.

At first Messe felt pressure only from Eighth Army as he ran for a delaying position on the Faid – Sfax road. But on the second night of the retreat – that of April 7/8 – robust movements by British infantry from behind French infantry positions to the west of Pichon announced the long feared threat of envelopment. By daylight some of the German troops had decamped and only a few low grade units blocked the vital Fondouk Pass – vital because, if it fell at once, nothing could prevent the IXth Corps overrunning the Kairouan Plain.

But luckily for the Axis neither the British nor the American infantry, committed to assaulting the pass and other territory to the north, had the requisite experience to advance over difficult ground, at speed, clearing opposition as they went. Furthermore, the extensive minefields and an anti-tank gun screen covering the approaches exacted a disproportionate toll upon the Anglo-Americans, made heavier by the headlong nature of a series of desperate charges. So a critical delay held back IXth Corps, preventing its armour from getting free until the morning of April 10.

By then Afrika Korps had arrived and mostly, in fact, passed on its way north. Meanwhile the British, unsure of the location of the Axis main body, stood still and asked for further directions – directions that did not arrive until the evening; far too late, of course, for by then only fast retreating rearguards scudded across the plain in the direction of the looming hills surrounding Enfidaville. Apart from stragglers, First Italian Army had escaped, presaging a complete change in the subsequent conduct of operations.

Henceforward, mobility took second place to positional mountain warfare in the rugged terrain – such as Afrika Korps had never encountered before. A ring of hills encircled the essential ports and airfields grouped about Bizerta and Tunis, acting as a close knit complex that, as First British and Fifth Panzer Army knew, could be horribly costly to assault.

First Italian Army occupied the hills guarding the coastal approaches, retaining 90th and 164th Light with 15th Panzer, while Afrika Korps temporarily held a bulge in the line below Pont du Fahs. Thus, as the last act in North Africa began, Afrika Korps became divorced from its prime opponent, the veteran British Eighth Army, and opposed instead to a weak French Corps – the XIXth – the poorly equipped residue of an old fashioned army whose loyalty, until recently, had been sorely tried, politically. Only in the Medjerda Valley could country be found in which mechanised forces might perform with speed and decision, and it was towards this area that the more mobile element of Afrika Korps, shortly to be followed by its headquarters, began to go.

Yet simply to move forces from one front to another (let alone keep them mobile once they got there) raised logistic problems which could no longer be solved. For weeks Army Group Afrika had contrived to operate on the lowest imaginable consumption. On March 31, First Italian Army, poised between mobile actions, could lay its hands on barely 40 miles worth of petrol per vehicle (with no reserve within over 100 miles) and little more than two issues of ammunition. Fifth Panzer Army was if anything worse off and by the middle of the month the situation had deteriorated even further. Now the Allied Air Forces and the British Royal Navy clamped a stranglehold upon the supply routes. Imports no longer replaced consumption yet, paradoxically, men continued to be flown in. The Tunisian bridgehead wilted in a crazy muddle.

But, while the Axis leaders blindly declined to admit the utter hopelessness of the situation they had created in Tunisia, and turned deaf ears to the pleas by the field commanders on the spot to cut their losses, the hierarchy in Tunisia began subtly to salvage some of the most experienced amongst their number to fight again in Europe. Rommel's old ADC, Schmidt, was sent home to get married, several senior officers fell ill and others came home to attend conferences. This is not written, by any means, as criticism. Criticism, such as can be levelled under these circumstances is at a system which vainly sacrificed so many good soldiers just a few weeks after the cream of the German Army had been skimmed off at Stalingrad.

Shortly after Eighth Army arrived at Enfidaville it launched a heavy and persistent attack aimed to bludgeon a way past the mountain heights – and failed. Meantime a series of Allied attacks were launched along the length of the front, continuing unremittingly in varying degrees of intensity and magnitude from April 22. To von Arnim the fact that these attacks either took place in or around the Medjerda Valley came as no surprise. That valley, with its western end in Allied hands (even though its flanks were held by Germans) pointed a dagger at the heart of Axis resistance – Tunis.

By the beginning of May, despite a protest from Kesselring, von Arnim chose to concentrate his strongest forces in Medjerda – many from Afrika Korps, including the whole of its armour. Of course, moves such as these were utterly futile and by April 30 the German armour had shot its bolt, but in the most glorious way possible.

The chosen Allied thrust line, as von Arnim accurately forecasted, centred on the Medjerda Valley, although parallel thrusts by American troops to the north in the direction of Bizerta were to exert an important leverage in aid of the principal effort. By April 27 it looked as if the critical moment had arrived. The British had cleared the heights including the notorious Longstop Hill, and had seized the last barrier, Djebel Bou Aoukaz. Expecting an immediate exploitation, von Arnim brought every available surviving armoured detachment together under Colonel Irkens in 8th Panzer Regiment, that celebrated formation which had first fought in Afrika Korps during Operation 'Battleaxe'. But, since the British armour lay either behind Eighth Army or stoppered up in the Goubellat Plain, no exploitation took place.

Appreciating that the British infantry might be temporarily exhausted (as most certainly they were) and reflecting that, for this reason, the enemy would employ the next three days regrouping (as it habitually did prior to a fresh effort) von Arnim took 8th Panzer Regiment under his personal direction and flung it, on April 28, against Djebel Bou Aoukaz. The attack was fraught with peril and quite hopeless, yet this last valkyrian charge of Afrika Korps carried with it the hopes of spiritual salvation and an emotional farewell to combat. The order of battle of Irken's Battle Group thus assumed an almost mystical symbolism, comprising as it did, detachments from:—

5th Panzer Regiment (once in 5th Light later 21st Panzer Division),

7th Panzer Regiment (once in 10th Panzer Division),

8th Panzer Regiment (once in 15th Panzer Division),

one company 501 Panzer Battalion (Tiger tanks),

2nd Battalion 47th Grenadier Battalion,

C-in-C's escort (2½ platoons),

one anti-tank company,

one field battery,

two batteries of 88 mm anti-aircraft guns, and a few Italian tanks and guns.

Hurling itself with traditional skill and fury against Bou Aoukaz, this heterogeneous group achieved results of which Rommel himself would have been proud, and in the intense fighting that followed persisted to the point of exhaustion, on April 30, flinging the British off the Djebel.

And there Afrika Korps bowed out, its last action befitting its history. If it could have fought more it would have done so. In fact 69 tanks remained fit for battle in important details except that of petrol, so all the crews could do was await the end where they stood. Nor was that end long coming, for even as 8th Panzer Regiment faded from battle, General Alexander set in motion the final preparations to crush Army Group 'Afrika'.

The last camp for Afrika Korps. Prisoners in their thousands enter the cages in Tunisia

Balance sheet

Tiger I – Germany's latest and heaviest tank knocked out in Tunisia

On May 6, Alexander propelled a concentrated force comprising of the 7th Armoured and 4th Indian Divisions, 201st Guards Brigade, (from Enfidaville) and 4th British Infantry and 6th Armoured Division (from the head of the Medjerda Valley), towards Tunis, completing this advance with a rolling aerial and artillery bombardment of staggering dimensions. Nothing could withstand the pressure of attack and in truth, little enough aspired to attempt to do so. Twenty-four hours later the whole Axis house of cards in Africa tumbled down.

Bizerta fell to the Americans, Tunis to the British. Here and there veteran Afrika Korps gun crews and grounded tankmen fought to the death, but mostly they congregated to surrender in the same fatalistic, orderly fashion which had persuaded their opponents to respect them all along. As the fighting men and their officers, tramped stolidly into captivity in marshalled formation, they held themselves with a dignity of which all took note in solid admiration.

Unfortunately, in an excess of ponderous zeal, General von Arnim let his side down. Retiring with his headquarters and that of General Cramer into a mountain retreat, he determined to carry the point of resistance to extremes by destroying all his signal equipment in order to avoid ordering his men to surrender. It made not the slightest difference except to reduce von Arnim's dignity to a level far below that of his soldiers. Waiting until the British overlooked his headquarters and that of Afrika Korps, von Arnim, with Cramer at his side, haggled with the British senior commanders; but in the midst found himself ignominiously looking a Gurkha commanding officer and his escort in the face at a somewhat alarming range.

Valedictory messages had already passed between the Axis groups and the Fatherland, Cramer's last message going to Rommel in convalescence in Austria, where he reflected that at least his 'Africans' in captivity, would be spared the coming holocaust in Europe. Cramer's last formal message to Army Group 'Afrika' and the High Command in Germany, closed Afrika Korps' life on a typically defiant note of hope:

'Ammunition shot off. Arms and equipment destroyed. In accordance with orders received DAK has fought itself to the condition where it can fight no more. The German Afrika Korps must rise again.

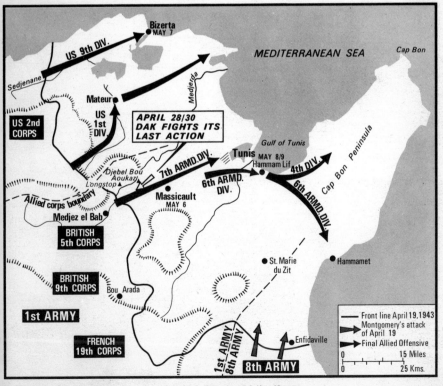

Tunisia: the end. But there is no Dunkirk for the Afrika Korps

157

General von Arnim enters captivity

Heia Safari. Cramer, General Commanding'
What had they achieved?

First, beyond doubt a reputation second to none – that well worn military catch-phrase which in this case really does indicate the apex of achievement. Lifted to extraordinary feats of endurance by Rommel (whose name and prestige are, after all, synonymous with Afrika Korps) this unique formation in a comparatively short time acquired a fiercesome image that helped it win battles against superior numbers on the strength of prestige alone. Better still, it achieved this profound respect from its opponents with a bearing, skill and chivalry that outranked anything to be found on any other battlefield of the Second World War. There was no wave of premeditated atrocities in the desert, and Rommel and Afrika Korps were as one with their opponents in stamping on the slightest cause for their inception.

In technique and equipment, the German Army in Africa retained an edge, in many aspects, to the bitter end, and did so with the most astonishing improvisations. For this reason they educated the Anglo-American forces in much that subsequently became common practice to the end of the war. Eighth Army even took over one of Afrika Korps' favourite songs, 'Lili Marlene' and sang it in competition. Thus far, therefore, the balance sheet stands boldly in Afrika Korps' favour.

On the surface its most striking and dramatic victories also stand on the credit side, masterpieces parallel with the others inflicted by German Arms in almost every campaign from 1939 to mid-1942. But after 1942, the balance becomes less easy to assess since, of all the Axis victories, those in the Western Desert were on occasion – and certainly at the beginning – the least welcome, because, by their political and propaganda implications, they deflected Axis strategy from its considered course.

Hitler would much rather not have had need to disperse his striking force to assist his ailing Italian partner, and therefore looked on the Afrika Korps only as a political prop to shore up a rotten organisation. Unless Germany was prepared to turn North Africa into a major seat of war, taking over the coastline from Casablanca to Port Said while subjugating Malta, no sizeable land force could operate other than at the end of a shoe-string. That Hitler could have achieved such a large-scale take-over in 1941 (instead of going into Russia), there can be little doubt – particularly when the scale of the last minute performance in Tunisia is taken into account. Whether he could have maintained it is another matter.

But Hitler, like Napoleon, always boggled at the sight and sound of the sea, and the Mediterranean puzzled him in the same way as the English Channel. And so Afrika Korps dragged him reluctantly but ever-deeper into the African continent, and by the very magnitude of its success, signed its own death warrant and also became a major factor in shaping Axis and British strategy.

Conjecture can often be a fruitless pastime, but let us indulge in it just for a moment. Supposing Afrika Korps, not led by the unconventional and aggressive Rommel, had adopted and maintained a defensive posture from the beginning, as desired by Halder and as practised by Wavell in Cyrenaica. With the calamitous events in Greece, the upheavals in the Middle East and then the German eruption into Russia, would the British have thrown their effort westwards towards Tripoli, or is it not more likely that they would have sought means to come to Russia's direct aid through 'the soft underbelly of Europe'? Judged by the alacrity with which Britain had rushed into Greece and her vital need to secure the Middle East oilfields, we may discount a strong westward move before 1943 at the earliest.

Next, suppose that later in 1941 Rommel had taken the offensive and failed without exciting too much jubilation on the British part. Would not the British have been able to take a more sanguine view of the Middle East and conserve its central reserve for use elsewhere? Is it not possible that Afrika Korps acted as a magnet out of all proportion to its size, and lured extravagant resources far from Britain into a campaign that became a battle of prestige as well as of wits?

Recall some other select, professional bands which, in the past, rejected the conventional and swept mightier hosts before them time and again. Think of David, the Greeks and Spartans, the English archers in France, John Zizka's tiny Hussite mobile wagon laagers, a host of outnumbered revolutionary armies from Washington's to Gariboldi's and – right up-to-date – the Israelis in Sinai. Finally, remember the fate of these catalysts once their strength had subsided and they became consumed by the fate of respectability.

In the last analysis, however, it is the quality of the men – and above all the man at the top – which counts most. In this respect Afrika Korps was doubly fortunate in its leader and the way he outwitted his opponents for nearly two years. It is the measure of Afrika Korps' achievement that even when pitted against warriors as doughty and steadfast as themselves, they fought clean right to the bitter end.

Bibliography

The author is grateful to Allen and Unwin Ltd, for permission to quote from 'Alamein – an Italian Story' by Caccia-Dominioni and George G Harrap and Co Ltd, for permission to quote from 'With Rommel in the Desert' by H W Schmidt

Alamein–an Italian Story Caccia-Dominioni (Allen & Unwin, London)
The Rommel Papers ed B H Liddell Hart (Cassell, London. Harcourt, Brace, New York)
The Tanks B H Liddell Hart (Cassell, London. Praeger, New York)
The Other Side of the Hill B H Liddell Hart (Cassell, London. Liddell Hart, New York)
With Rommel in the Desert H W Schmidt (Harrap, London)
Purnell's History of the Second World War ed B H Liddell Hart & B Pitt
The Mediterranean and Middle East, Vols. I to IV 150 Playfair and others (HMSO, London)
New Zealand in the Second World War, Bardia to Enfidaville W G Stevens (NZ War History Branch, Wellington NZ)
Crisis in the Desert Agar Hamilton (Oxford University Press, Cape Town)
Seizing the Initiative G F Howe (Office of the Chief of Military History, Department of the Army, Washington)
Soldier to the Last Day (US: *A Soldier's Record*) Field Marshal Albert Kesselring (William Kimber, London. Morrow, New York)
Rommel Desmond Young (Collins, London. Harper & Row, New York)